The Ups and Downs of Needlepoint

Frontispiece Rose is a Rose. 10½ x 8 in. on #10 canvas. Worked by Betsy Wiederhold (Graph 1)

Graph 1 Rose is a Rose . . . on **#10** graph. Adaptation by permission of the estate of **Gertrude Stein** (**Frontispiece**)

The Ups and Downs

of

Needlepoint

FANNIE HILLSMITH

SOUTH BRUNSWICK AND NEW YORK: A. S. BARNES AND COMPANY
LONDON: THOMAS YOSELOFF LTD

A. S. Barnes and Co., Inc.
Cranbury, New Jersey 08512

Thomas Yoseloff Ltd
108 New Bond Street
London W1Y OQX, England

Library of Congress Cataloging in Publication Data

Hillsmith, Fannie.
    The ups and downs of needlepoint.

    Includes index.
    1. Canvas embroidery. I. Title.
TT778.C3H54 1975   746.4′4   73-147
ISBN 0-498-01336-7

Unless otherwise noted, all drawings, designs, black and white photographs, color plates, and needlepoint are by the author.

PRINTED IN THE UNITED STATES OF AMERICA

For Irma,
who titled the book

Contents

Preface

In FINE ARTS, where it is the artist's idea, good or bad, that counts, technique often takes second place. This can cause disastrous results.

In CRAFTS the opposite seems to be the rule, and skill of execution often takes priority over good design. It almost seems that the worse the design, the more one can parade one's technique.

Needlepoint appears to be one of the major sufferers and lies fallow in a sea of spent florals, arch animals, and just general indifference to composition, which is not relieved in the least by the sterile, too rigid patterns that seem to be coming to the fore today. This does not apply to the marvelous quilt designs of the past that are so alive with their fool-the-eye perspective and unwavering sense of design.

Of course, there are isolated experts, but *only* with a more critical attitude in a wider area can needlepoint design improve generally and rise to a more aware and sensitive level.

The purpose of this book is twofold:

1. To present a basic, step-by-step approach in the correct way to do the Continental and basket weave stitches and show how to "draw" shapes with the needle. (These two stitches combine well and are best for this book, where the accent is on design.)

2. To show how to make your own designs and thereby experience a most satisfying feeling—that is, the triumph of your own composition coming to life in a fresh, new image.

I Couldn't Have Done It without the Help of . . .

In the Fine Arts world, the artist, writer, composer, or pianist has to go it alone. It is his or her problem that has to be solved *alone*.

In the Oscar awards it becomes a little bewildering when the actors name a long list of all the people who made their Academy Awards possible—that is, until you yourself undertake the writing, illustrations, diagrams, and photography of a book! Then you know why.

So I too say, I couldn't have done this book without the help of Irma Royce, my secretary and adviser; Vivian Campbell Stoll and Jeanette Barker, with their helpful comments; Lilo Ganshorn, with her ingenuity and consistency in executing my designs on graph paper; and Betsy Wiederhold, who executed the most intricate of my needlepoints. I thank them, and also Elisabeth Sears of the Needlewoman's Shop in Duxbury, Massachusetts, for her inexhaustible advice, and Stella Scott and Mary Fulton for helping in the final stages.

I also want to thank Evelyn Ruffle, the Jaffrey, New Hampshire, librarian; Frederick Richardson of the Village Shop; and the Free Library in Duxbury, Massachusetts.

I must mention the kindness of Museum people: Jean Mailey of the Metropolitan Museum of Art; Biri Fay of the Brooklyn Museum; Lorraine Turner of the Boston Museum of Fine Arts; Alfred J. Wyatt of the Philadelphia Museum of Fine Arts; and Donald Gallup of the Beinecke Rare Book and Manuscript Library at Yale University Library. And I am grateful for the cooperation of European museums, whose curators responded with such enthusiastic letters in French and German!

And last of all, I thank the publisher, Julien Yoseloff, who gave me free rein on my subject matter and my ideas, and my editor, Mathilde Finch.

The Ups and Downs
of
Needlepoint

1
Needlepoint

Needlepoint is "working" stitches on a kind of open-weave canvas, made up of fibrous threads that, because they are separated, form meshes.

A MESH is a hole surrounded by warp (horizontal) and woof (vertical) canvas threads.

The number of holes to the inch determines the size of the canvas. For example, 10 holes to the inch would be called 10-inch canvas, or #10 canvas, or 10 point.

The size of the canvas determines the size of the needle and the number of strands to be used at a time (Fig. 1).

In threading the needle (Fig. 2), bury the loop between your thumb and forefinger so it is firm enough to go through the needle easily.

MONO canvas has single threads, and PENELOPE has double threads (Fig. 3 a, b).

ALWAYS have the selvage on the side of your working canvas.

You will notice in the penelope that the woof threads are much closer together than the warp.

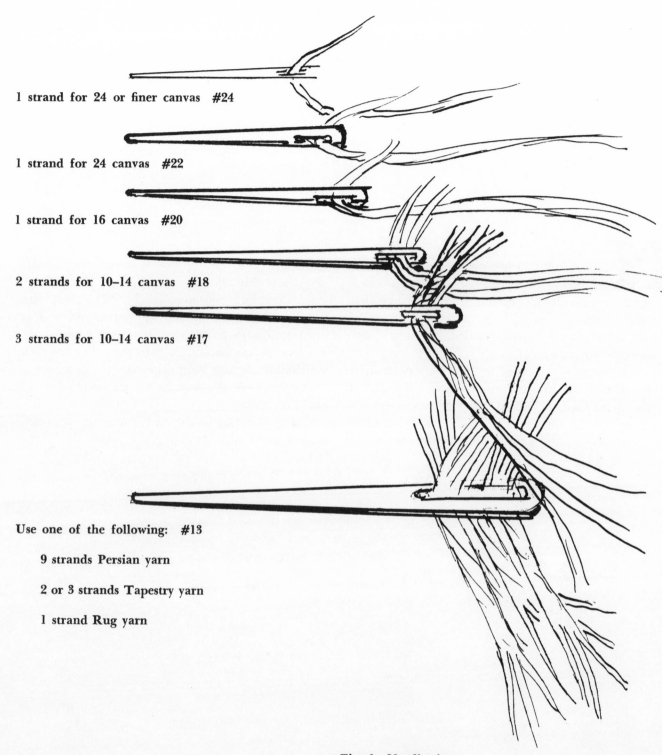

1 strand for 24 or finer canvas #24

1 strand for 24 canvas #22

1 strand for 16 canvas #20

2 strands for 10–14 canvas #18

3 strands for 10–14 canvas #17

Use one of the following: #13

    9 strands Persian yarn

    2 or 3 strands Tapestry yarn

    1 strand Rug yarn

Fig. 1 Needle sizes

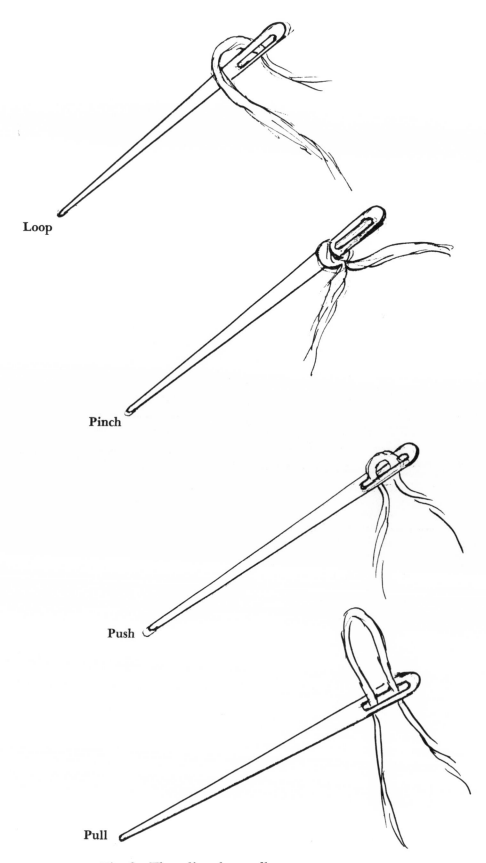

Loop

Pinch

Push

Pull

Fig. 2   Threading the needle

17

2
What Is a Stitch?

A stitch is a length of yarn that wraps around the intersection of the threads (Fig. 3 c).

It *always* slants like the accent aigu over an *é* or like five past seven o'clock [/] and is always worked in *horizontal* rows on the canvas in the Continental and *diagonally* in the basket weave.

The wool for the stitching is usually Persian yarn made up of three strands that may be separated. On #10 canvas, two strands should be sufficient, though sometimes three are needed to cover the canvas, particularly in a dark color. The shorter the strand, the less the wear and tear, because drawing the yarn through the canvas weakens it and makes it thin.

Whereas half of this book is concerned about where the needle comes UP, there is ALWAYS only ONE place for the needle to go DOWN, diagonally to the right, to complete the stitch (Fig. 3, f).

In needlepoint parlance one always refers to the stitchery as "working" a canvas.

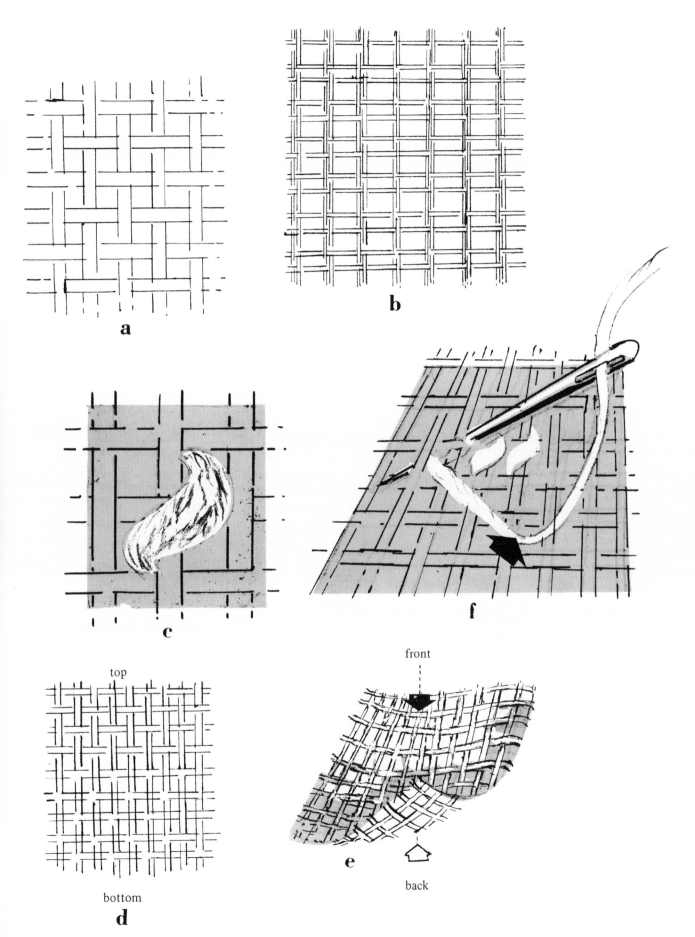

a

b

c

f

top

bottom

d

front

back

e

Fig. 3   Mono and penelope

19

3
Mono and Penelope

For a beginner I strongly advise mono canvas (see chapter 7, The Continental or Tent). It's a good way to become used to the relationship of the openings in the canvas. *It is very important to be aware of the diagonals.* Sometimes in an area surrounded by already-worked canvas, it can be confusing to know where one *is,* to know where the next horizontal, vertical, or diagonal is.

I advise beginners to make a lot of circles. It is good practice in becoming aware of the relationship of the square openings.

As one progresses, one may still fight the penelope because of the multiple canvas threads. But suddenly it will seem perfectly simple, and much more satisfying. For one thing, penelope holds its shape much better than the mono. And of course it permits the possibility of combining petit point and gros point, which becomes more and more intriguing as you become more expert.

Tinkle, a Cat, Plate I (also Fig. 4, Graphs 2a and b and 3a and b, photograph detail 1), with his head worked in petit point, shows how penelope canvas opens up many possibilities in areas where detail is needed.

I have always been vaguely unhappy over the way a petit-point shape nestles down into the gros point surrounding it, so I have made designs where the petit point extends beyond the subject into a pattern of its own. In this instance the shape is hexagonal.

Plates II and III are quick point penelope (only 5 squares to the inch, which creates larger stitches.) They are worked in different color versions of the same design (Graph 4).

An artist friend, James Zeigler, who worked Heraldry #2, went a step further. He made a real innovation by reversing the normal procedure and making the subject (the lion) gros point and the background petit point! In this way the subject is predominant, rather than lost in the gros point (Plate III).

In the case of the two butterflies, Plates IV and V, the first is on penelope and the second on mono canvas. In either case it would have been superfluous to use petit point.

In studying some of the graph drawings in this book you will find variations on this interesting problem. Try to think of solutions, yourself, to this situation.

Fig. 4   Photostat of Tinkle

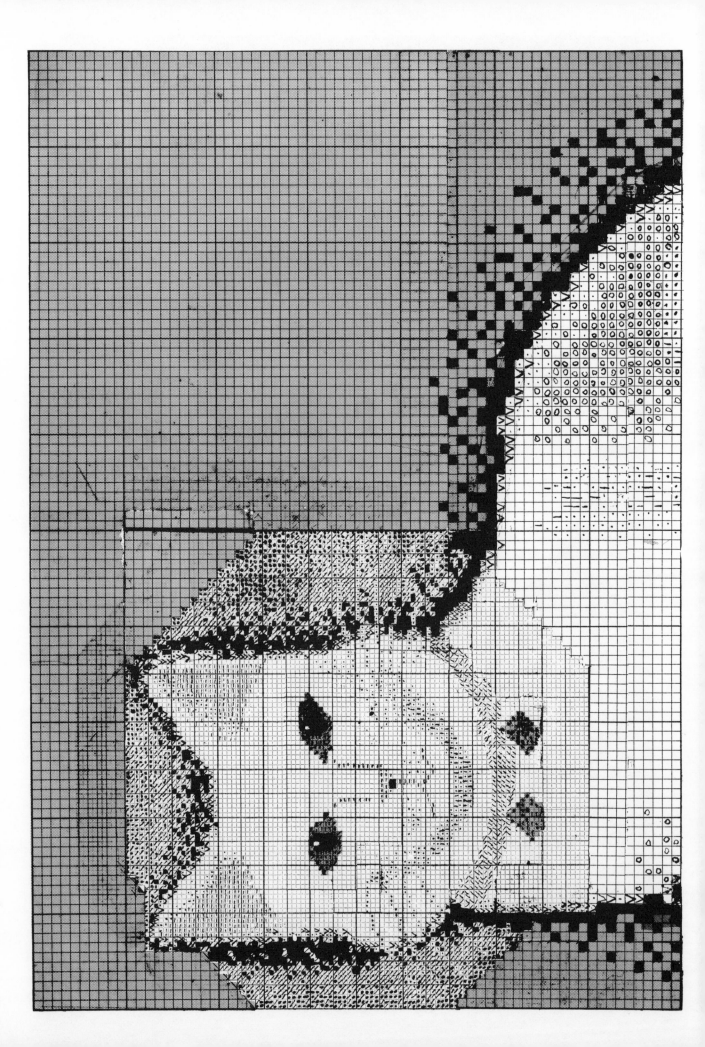

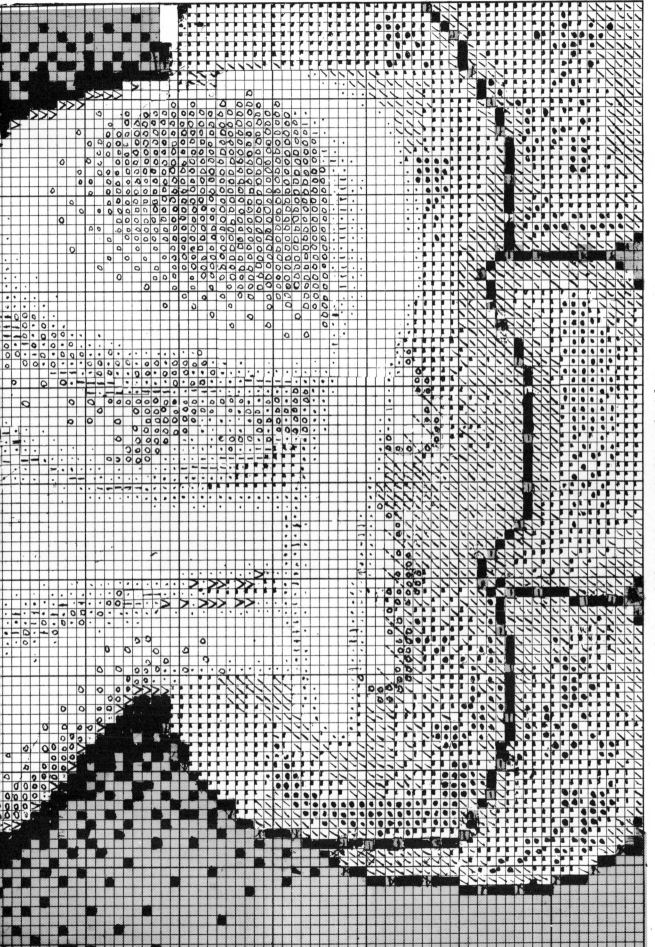

Graphs 2a and 2b Tinkle on #10/20 graph. Adaptation from the American Primitive painting, Tinkle. Collection of Shelburne Museum, Inc., Shelburne, Vermont (Fig. 4, Plate I)

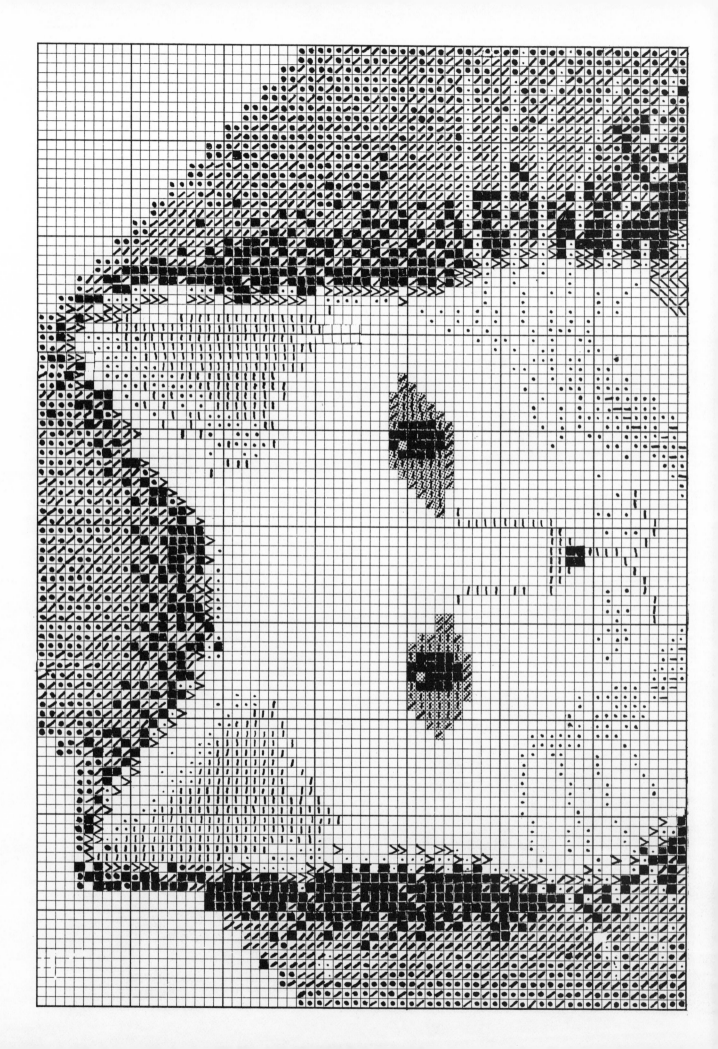

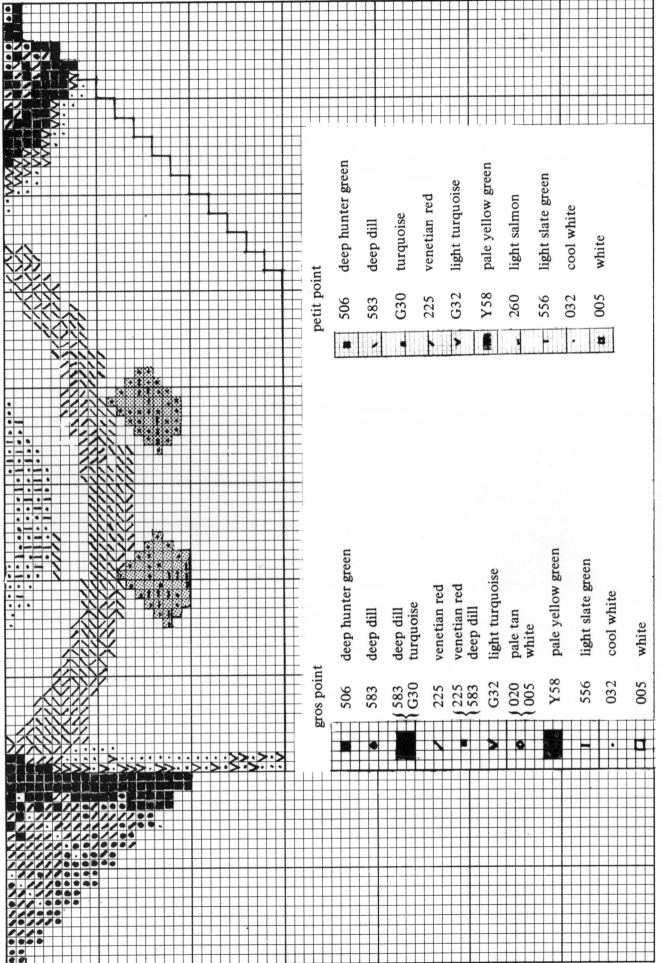

petit point

506	deep hunter green
583	deep dill
G30	turquoise
225	venetian red
G32	light turquoise
Y58	pale yellow green
260	light salmon
556	light slate green
032	cool white
005	white

gros point

506	deep hunter green
583	deep dill
583 G30	deep dill / turquoise
225	venetian red
225 583	venetian red / deep dill
G32	light turquoise
020 005	pale tan / white
Y58	pale yellow green
556	light slate green
032	cool white
005	white

Graphs 3a and 3b Tinkle on #10/20 graph. Detail
(Photograph 1)

Photograph 1 Detail of Tinkle. Petit-point area
(Graphs 3a, 3b, Plate I)

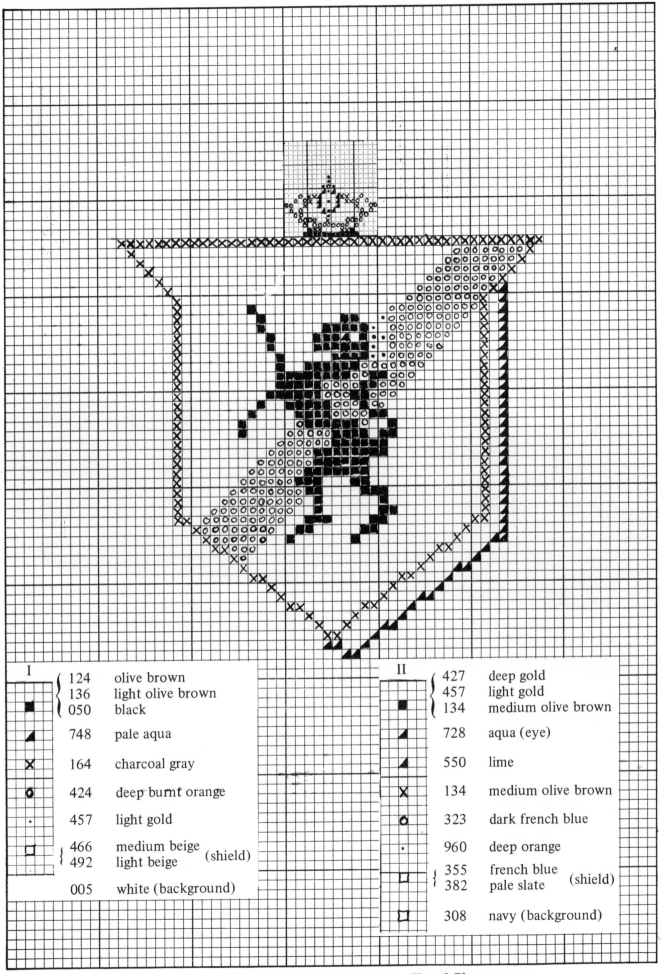

I			
	{	124	olive brown
■	{	136	light olive brown
	{	050	black
◢		748	pale aqua
✕		164	charcoal gray
⊙		424	deep burnt orange
•		457	light gold
⊡	{	466	medium beige (shield)
	{	492	light beige
		005	white (background)

II			
	{	427	deep gold
■	{	457	light gold
	{	134	medium olive brown
◢		728	aqua (eye)
◢		550	lime
✕		134	medium olive brown
⊙		323	dark french blue
•		960	deep orange
⊡	{	355	french blue (shield)
	{	382	pale slate
⊡		308	navy (background)

Graph 4 **Heraldry on #10 graph (Plate II and Plate III for two color variations)**

4
From Kits to Mitts

If you are a novice and have a desire to start with an already-designed canvas, look for simple, fresh, open designs like these painted canvases by Betsy Borden, Plate XI.

In buying a canvas with a painted design you will have cooperation from the shop, whose assistant will help you get started and pick your yarn for you.

Except for what is available in museums, where needlepoint kits are based on a good source usually drawn from their own collections, my advice is to stay away from the kit form of assemblage, which is expensive and commercial with routine subject matter and indifferent design.

Try some very simple designs like First Attempts, Plates XII, XIII, and XIV. After all, there is nothing more sophisticated than stripes and squares. Go to any modern gallery to discover this. Plate XV is an expert example of a simple idea.

Some shops and mail-order houses seem carried away with way-out things to make—from a Christmas stocking that would take weeks to execute to a toothbrush cover and golf-club mitt. This seems a desperate means for achieving something new.

As you become more proficient, you can strike out on your own, with not only the satisfaction of realizing your own ideas but also the economy of narrowing down expenses to wool and canvas.

Start on stripes as suggested in chapter 5. Then work slowly toward more intricate designs, beginning with simple outlines of flowers and animals such as Small Motifs (Graph 5) and Miniatures from the Met (Graph 6). (The topmost creature in Small Motifs you will meet again in chapter 40, Your First Design.)

Graph 5 Small Motifs on #20 graph. Adaptations
from samplers at the Metropolitan Museum of Art

Graph 6 Miniatures from the Met on #20 graph. Adaptations from samplers at the Metropolitan Museum of Art

5
Diehards

Diehards will give any excuse for not doing their own designs. If they work, they are tired at the end of the day and about all the energy they can summon up is to drop into a needlepoint shop and pick up a kit and select the required yarns. By the time they get home they are filled with the cozy feeling of accomplishment-about-to-happen.

The different levels of creativity cannot be overstressed. Not only in the various ranges of people with talent, but in each person, there are some times when there seem to be more ideas than at others.

For instance, why not set aside a couple of hours on the weekend, make your design, transpose it to graph paper or canvas, and plan to work the large areas during the week when you are tired or watching T.V. Generally, designs should be worked from the center out, so have several things going at once, like a pillow, a coaster, a doorstop cover. Suggestions for other designs to make are found in chapter 50, The Tailored Look. Not the least of these are needlepoint pictures themselves, a greatly overlooked art, partly due to the terrible imitation "painting" and frames popularly displayed before the public.

For an end-of-the-day suggestion when you are tired and have nothing planned, try this Simple Design (Graph 7) made up of only two colors and one dash of black. After you have indicated the shapes on the canvas, it is an easy matter to carry them out. If you become bored with too-large areas of one color, add stripes. See Plates XIV, XV, XVI, XX for ideas on stripes.

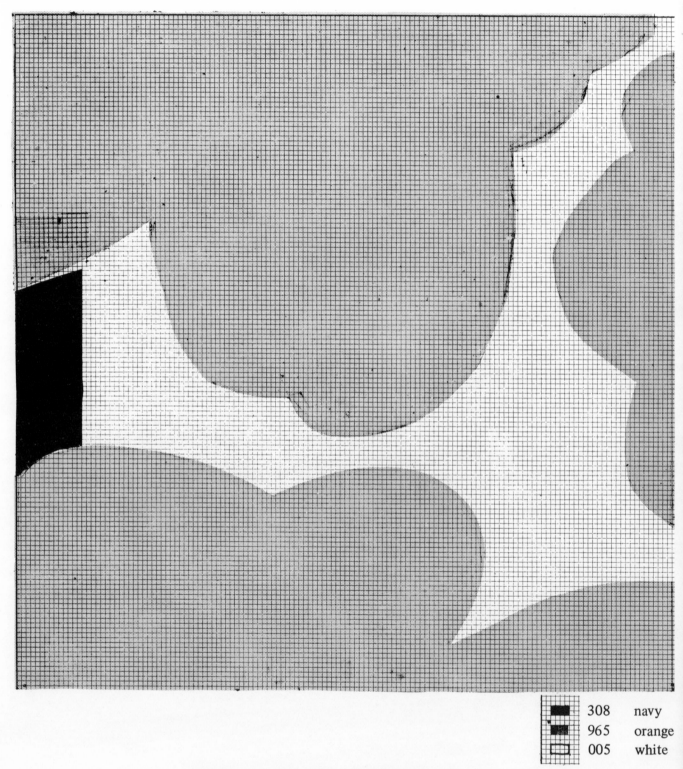

▪▪	308	navy
▨▨	965	orange
▢	005	white

Graph 7 **A Simple Design on #20 graph. Adaptation from a Marimekko Fabric Design Research**

Plate I Tinkle, a Cat. 14 x 10 in. on #10/20 canvas.
Worked by Betsy Wiederhold (Graphs 2a, 2b) (Fig. 4,
photostat enlargement)

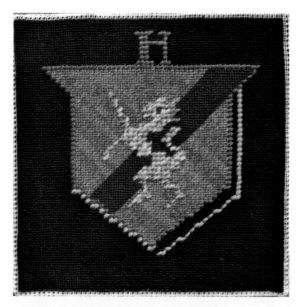

Plate II Heraldry I. 12 x 12 in. on #5 canvas. Worked by David Putnam (Graph 4)

Plate III Heraldry II. 12 x 12 in. on #5 canvas. Worked by James Ziegler (Graph 4)

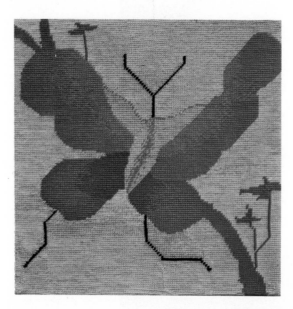

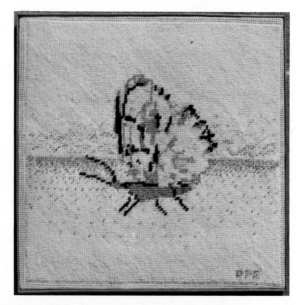

Plate IV Butterfly. 14 x 14 in. on #12 canvas. Designed and worked by Pamela Mattingly (Graph 50)

Plate V The White Butterfly. 12 x 12 in. on #10 canvas. Worked by Rachel Evans (Graph 46)

6
Dealing with Mistakes

Certainly the most important thing to remember in pulling out mistakes is *not to cut the canvas*. This would be a major disaster. You can add a swatch of canvas basted under the injury and weave it in with regular needlepoint stitches, but it's very difficult. Much better to exercise extreme caution.

Only *snip* at mistakes in the daytime under strong light and graze the stitches gingerly with a sharp pair of pointed scissors or a seam ripper *from the back* of the canvas, easing your way down to the canvas. Pull the stitches out *from the front* with fingers or tweezers.

If you have made a small error and want to backtrack a few stitches, pull gently on the wool from the back and you will see where to retract the needle.

7
The Continental or Tent

Song of the Needle (No. 1)

Even Steven, even Steven
UP is odd, DOWN is even.

Now let us begin. In the following diagrams, it is very important to remember that on the ODD numbers the threaded needle comes up from *underneath* the canvas through a square hole to the top and then goes back down through another hole (diagonally to the right) to the bottom on an EVEN number.

Mono canvas, 10 squares to the inch, is good to start with. Cut a piece 6½ inches square and fold ¾″ masking tape over the edges to keep it from raveling. *Selvage must always be on the right- or left-hand side,* not on the top or bottom. Draw a 3½″ square in the middle with a pencil or NEPO marker.

(If this turns out well on your first go, you can make it into a coaster!)

Draw some 1″ squares at random. Now thread needle with a length of 2 strands of yarn not more than 18″ long or 1 strand doubled over; knot thread and go from the front down to the back through a square about an inch from where you are going to start (Fig. 5). (When this is eventually covered up with stitches you can clip knot.) After a little practice omit the knot and simply leave the end of the yarn (½″) on the

front surface of the canvas, clipping it flush with canvas as needle approaches.

Start at the upper right-hand corner of your square and follow diagram slowly and carefully, pulling thread *gently but firmly*. (Keep your first piece so you can see signs of improvement.) Keep checking the back side, which can be very telltale if stitching isn't going well.

After your needle has gone UP on 1, DOWN on 2, UP on 3, DOWN on 4, and so forth, on the tenth stitch go DOWN on 20 (Fig. 6, a,b,c).

TURN CANVAS SO BOTTOM is at TOP.

UP on 21, DOWN on 22, UP on 23, and so forth. On the tenth stitch, UP on 39, DOWN on 40 (Fig. 6, d, e and Fig. 7, f).

TURN CANVAS. (Now TOP is again at top.)

Start all over again—UP on 1, DOWN on 2 (Fig. 7, g, h). Continue in this manner until you have done 10 rows (Fig. 6, i). DOWN on the last stitch. Slip yarn under a few stitches and clip (Fig. 7).

Now you have completed a square.

When you become familiar with where the stitches go, you can go up and down in one move, as in sewing.

Make several squares in different colors. You might put your initials in one of them (Plate XIII).

You will notice that on these small squares consisting of 10 stitches, the first stitch always

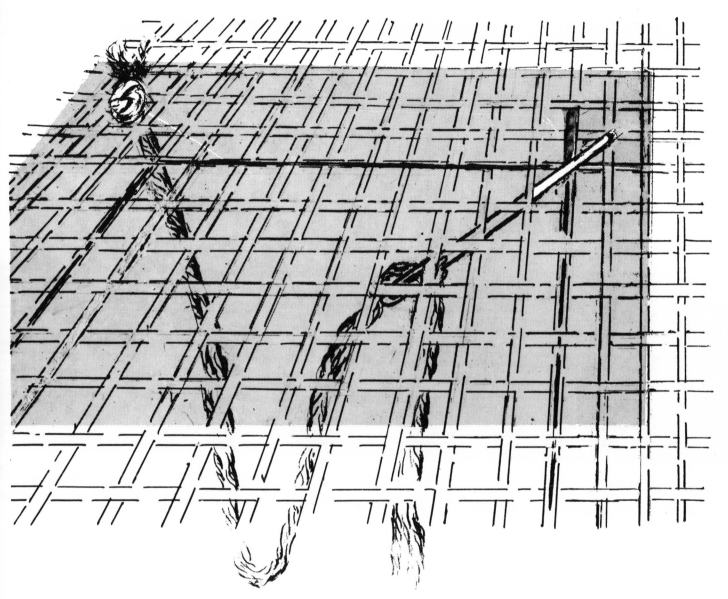

Fig. 5 First step

encompasses the drawn line and the 10th stitch just comes up to the second line, also the top line is covered and the bottom line exposed. This is the nature of the stitch.

If you did a series of 10-stitch squares, one after the other, you would realize why this is. It is because 11 stitches would cover the first square but throw the following squares off.

All arrows designate the TOP; always turn canvas to comply with arrow, but do *not* turn the book unless you are left-handed (see chapter 17).

NOTE: When NUMBERS and LETTERS are upside down, turn *both* book and canvas upside down.

Study figures *carefully* to see exactly which hole the needle comes UP in relation to other stitches and lines of the squares.

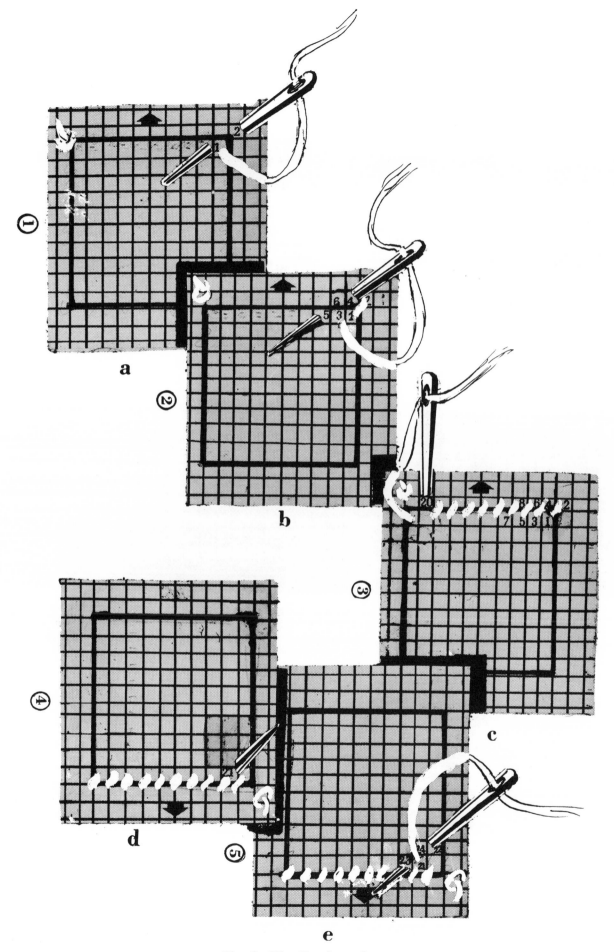

Fig. 6   The Continental or tent

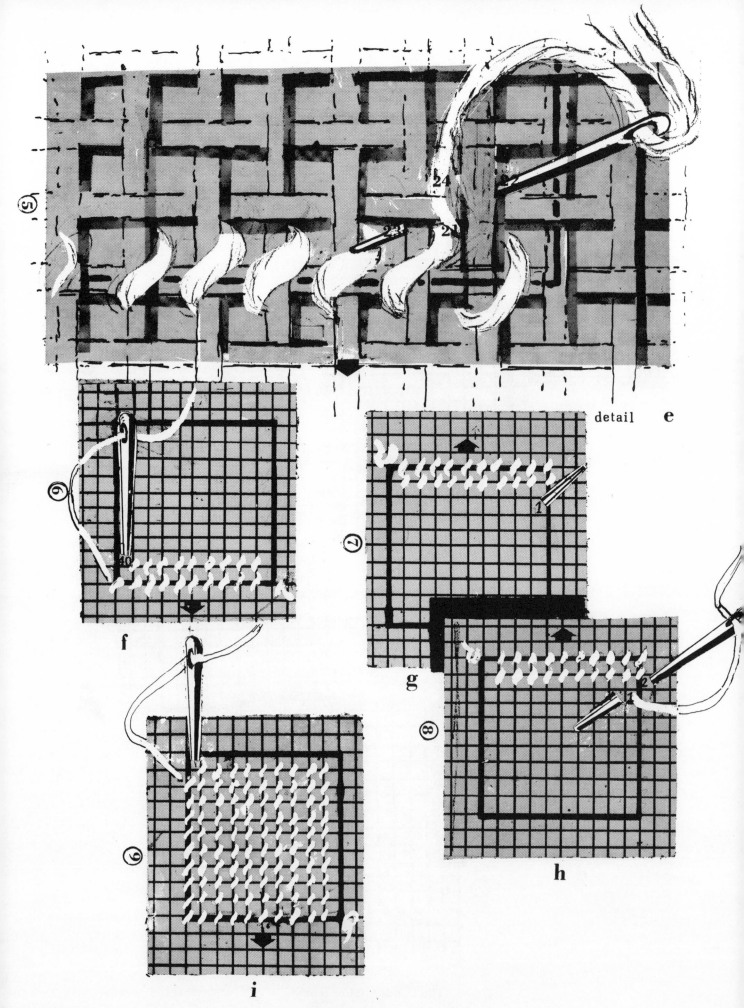

detail   **e**

f   **g**

h

i

Fig. 7   More Continental

8
The Direction of the Continental Stitch

Song of the Needle (No. 2)

To be truly UPRIGHT for a person is fine
But UP, RIGHT in needlepoint will worsen design.
So remember this rule and never lose sight:
To never go UP and never go RIGHT.

It is important to establish the two UPS and DOWNS of needlepoint.

1. UP and DOWN of the needle *through* the canvas, back to front, front to back as you sew (Fig. 3e).

2. UP and DOWN the surface of the canvas as you pursue the design from top to bottom (Fig. 3d).

In the Continental stitch you can go DOWN the canvas vertically and to the LEFT horizontally. But you cannot go UP the canvas vertically or to the RIGHT horizontally, so you have to turn it completely around so that UP becomes DOWN and going RIGHT becomes going LEFT.

In order to make it possible to follow a design that goes up or to the right, you must turn the canvas completely around.

If you don't believe that you can't go UP or to the RIGHT, try it and then look at the back. It looks thin. One would be amazed at the number of "pros" who don't know this.

If you are feeling confused by now, just memorize the jingle at the top.

Always remember that in going around a shape you are going LEFT, DIAGONALLY in any direction, and DOWN. There is absolutely no other way to go. Whenever you feel that you are not following these rules, you will suddenly realize that you are on a diagonal. Diagonals can be subtle, particularly when they are only two at a time. Always let the eye take in 2 or 3 squares beyond in your diagonal path. This will keep you in line.

After you have mastered the square and the circle, try diamonds and diagonals, Plates XVI

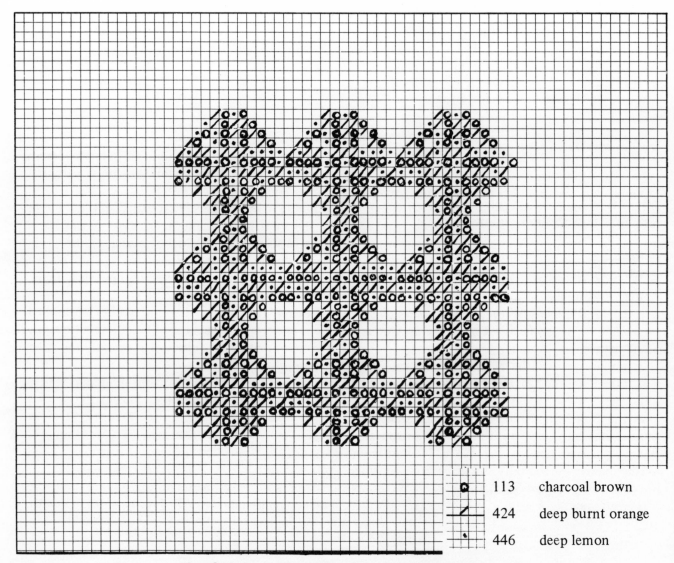

Graph 8 Caning on #10 graph. One version of a popular theme (Plate **XIX**)

and XVII. Finally branch out into more complex designs like semicircles and triangles (Plate XVIII) and caning (Graph 8, Plate XIX).

In an all-over design like caning, first establish the orange horizontals, then the verticals, and last the diagonals. Follow with the yellow in the same sequence and then with the dark brown. Finally, fill in with the background color.

9
The Basket-Weave Stitch

The basket-weave stitch, so named because of the basket-weave pattern on the back of the canvas, lies diagonally across the intersection of the canvas in the same manner as the Continental, but the *rows,* instead of going HORIZONTALLY to the left, travel DIAGONALLY, going DOWN and UP the surface of the canvas, with each row fitting into the other in coglike fashion (Fig. 9). The canvas, never turned upside down, stays in shape better than it does with the Continental. Often called a background stitch because of its suitability to large areas, the basket-weave stitch can, with experience, be worked into smaller shapes, and soon more detail, and more intricate detail, will be attempted. However, there is no strict rule about which stitch to use.

Practice many squares in both stitches to see what suits you best.

After you have mastered the square, try circles and ovals, which are the first step in filling in an uneven space, for rows will vary in length.

As you did for the Continental, cut a piece of 10 point canvas approximately 6" square, make a 3½" square in the center, and draw some 1" squares at random.

a. Start exactly as you did in the Continental. UP, DOWN, UP, with the 1st stitch encompassing an intersection of the canvas where the horizontal thread is uppermost, if you are using mono canvas (Fig. 8a).

b. On the 2nd DOWN stitch, position your needle vertically, going under stitch 1 as you complete another stitch at the TOP and start a 2nd below stitch 1 (Fig. 8b).

c. Complete the 2nd stitch and start the 3rd in a row that prepares you for the 2nd diagonal (Fig. 8c).

d. In completing the 3rd stitch, position your needle horizontally, preparatory to working diagonally up the canvas (Fig. 8d).

e. At the TOP, complete the diagonal and start the 4th stitch to the left. UP, DOWN, positioning the needle vertically for the next diagonal down the canvas (Fig. 8e).

f. Complete the diagonal and start the 5th stitch below the 4th, UP, DOWN with the needle in a horizontal position, preparatory for the next diagonal. Continue in this manner with the needle in *vertical* position working down and in *horizontal* working up (Fig. 8f).

g. In completing the square the last "row" will consist of 1 stitch UP, DOWN. Slip yarn under a few stitches and clip (Fig. 8g).

Notice that each time you end a diagonal row going up, you immediately make another stitch beside the last stitch at the top, and when you end a diagonal going down you make another stitch just below the last stitch. This puts you in line for each new diagonal row.

To make the square, on the 10th row, instead of extending the stitch start the next diagonal row *beside* the last stitch at the bottom and *below* the 10th stitch at the top.

Make your squares in different colors. Try some diagonal stripes, changing to another shade as your yarn runs out. If your squares were successful, fill in the background with a plain color and you will have another coaster!

NOTE: When running out of yarn, *end* and

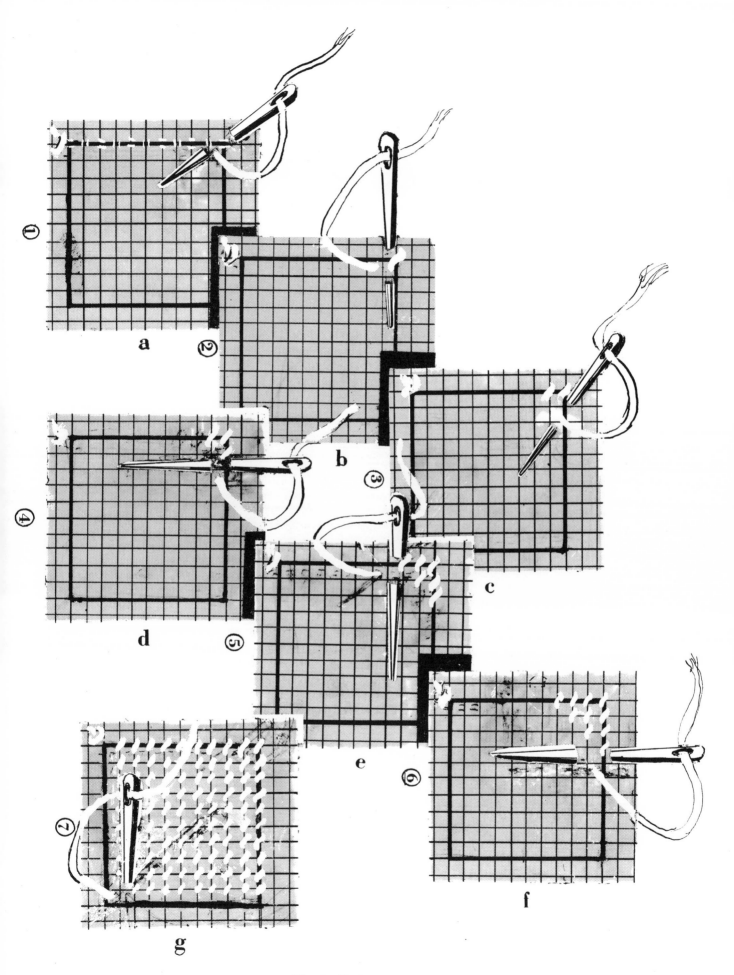

Fig. 8　Basket weave

start the same way as beginning and ending the square.

In the Continental, the needle is always at an angle until the end of the row, where it prepares for the next row.

Remember—there is always ONLY one place for the needle to go DOWN once you have established the UP.

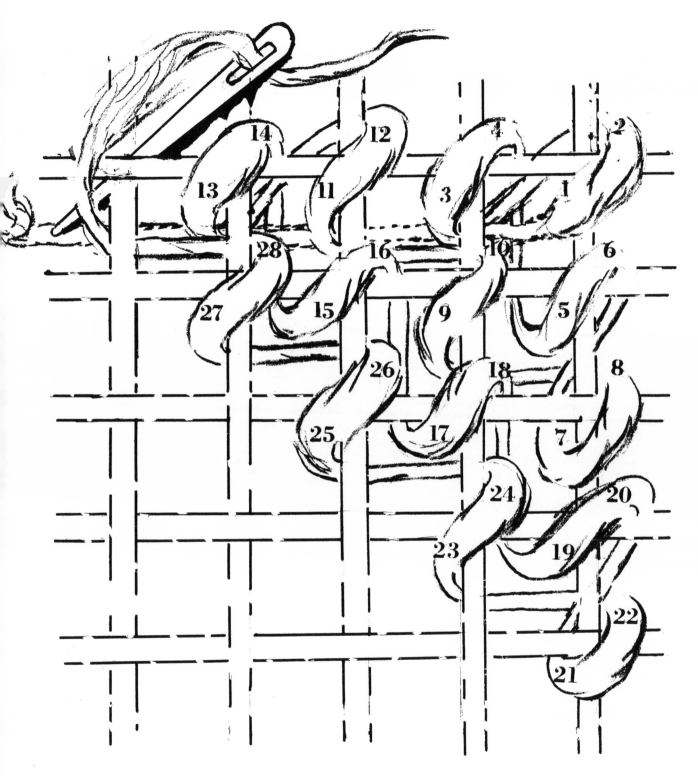

Fig. 9   More basket weave

10
Hazards of Basket Weave on Mono Canvas

Start the basket weave with a stitch at the very uppermost right-hand corner, encompassing an intersection of the canvas where the horizontal thread is uppermost (Fig. 10a). This gets the stitch in a proper position so that the needle is in a weaving relationship to the adjacent threads. In other words, it is *opposite* the thread on the right. If you study Figure 10 you will see why *a* is right and *b* is wrong.

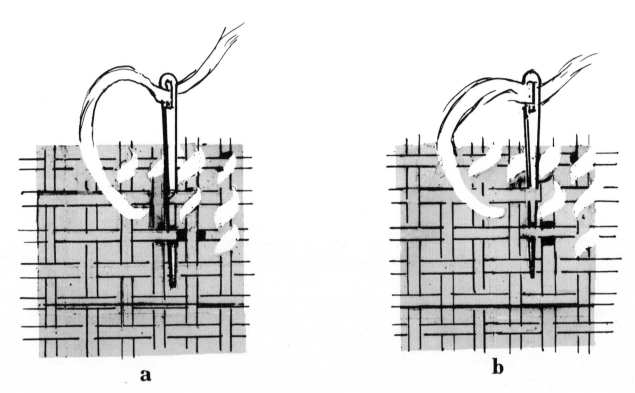

a   b

Fig. 10   Hazards of the basket weave

11
The Half Cross-Stitch

The half cross-stitch, so named because it is simply the *first half* of the cross-stitch and not a pure stitch, cannot function completely on its own.

It can only go back and forth horizontally (Fig. 11) but once it wants to go diagonally it must revert to the Continental.

Though not suitable for any piece requiring heavy wear because it is thin on the back, it is *ideal* for pictures, pillows, pin cushions, trivets, etcetera.

Unlike the Continental, the half cross goes from left to right and for this reason is most suit-able for the left-hander. However, some right-handers may find it pleasant going in this direc-tion and inserting the needle in a vertical position into the canvas, which is characteristic of this stitch.

Practice the three stitches, the Continental, basket weave, and half cross, to find out which feels most natural to you.

The half cross-stitch can only be worked on penelope.

Turn the canvas TOP to BOTTOM at the end of each odd row and right side up at the end of the even rows.

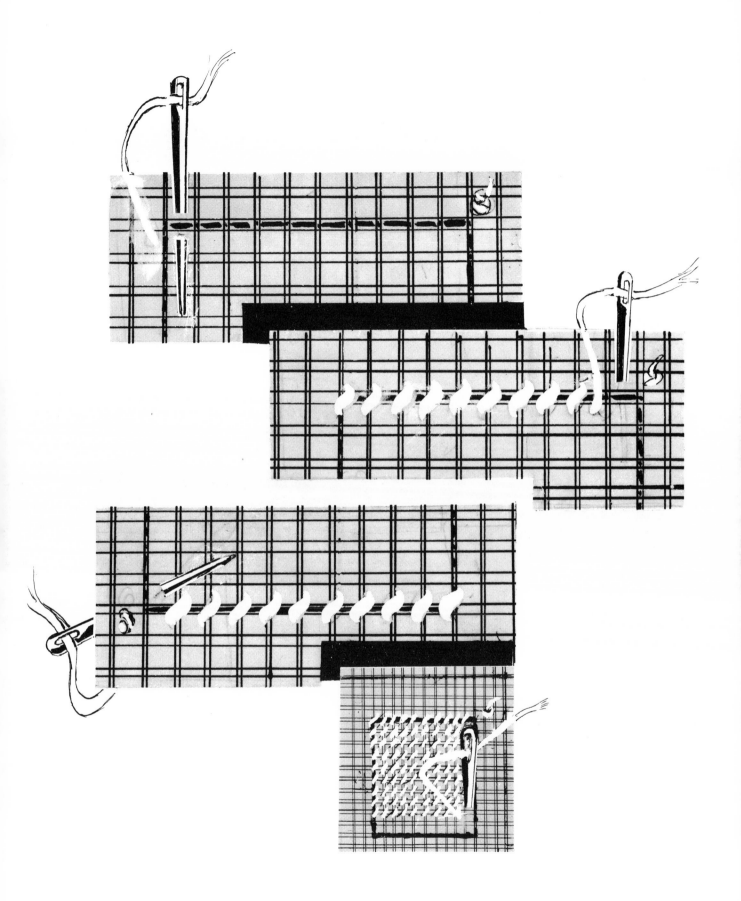

Fig. 11   The half cross-stitch

12
Tramé, and You Travel Fast

Tramé, an under stitch and a means of blocking-in your design, seems to be a forgotten process.

I think it has possibilities that have not been explored to their fullest. As with sketching a painting, freedom can be exercised because the long hemming stitches can cover territory fast and are also easy to remove in case of an error (Fig. 12).

Notice how the long stitches are spaced irregularly to make a more even padding for the needlepoint stitches to follow.

Half cross-stitch works very well on top of tramé, being a rather thin stitch itself.

Compare the backs of three stitches in Figure 13.

NOTE: In tramé, take short stitches so that most of the "basting" is on the top surface of the canvas. After traveling toward one side of the design, turn the canvas upside down and retrace your steps under the previous row to the side where you started.

Fig. 12   Tramé

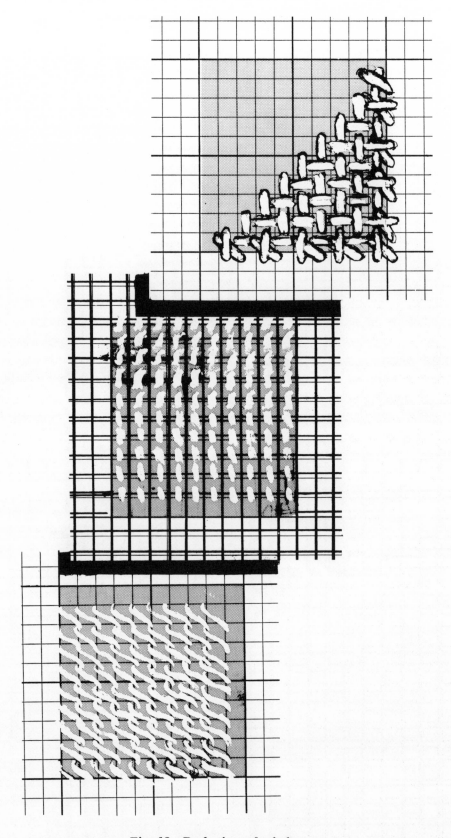

Fig. 13   Back view of stitches

13
Which Stitch?

hich stitch is best to use is a question often asked. A good basic rule in needlepoint is to use the Continental for the subject and the basket weave for the background. After you become more proficient you may *also* do the subject in basket weave, but it takes experience to fill in uneven shapes. (Try a circle first.)

The half cross is excellent over a design that has first been worked in tramé (see chapter 12). Being a thin stitch, it needs the padding of the horizontal thread of the tramé stitch. The half cross is almost a must for left-handers, but only on penelope or the new lockweave. (See chapter 55.)

14
Quick Point

Delightful and interesting as petit point is, I am a great advocate of quick point, done on #5 or #6 canvas.

It can be combined with 10 or 12 stitches to the inch by splitting the threads as in petit point. It goes very fast, is easy to see, therefore good to do at night, and is very effective combined with the smaller stitch.

Plates II, III, and XIV and Photograph 18e (see chapter 25, Motifs) are all needlepoint executed in quick point.

15
Advantages and Disadvantages of the Three Stitches (on #10 Canvas)

Continental (or Tent)

Advantages

Excellent for outlining and filling in shapes.

Has strong backing and wears well.

Can be worked on both mono and penelope canvas.

Good for both petit point and gros point.

Applicable for left-handers.

It takes about 20 minutes to work 1 square inch.

For working 1 square inch I average 2¼ yards (measured before doubling) of single-strand wool; 1½ yards of triple strands (as the Persian yarn comes) not doubled over.

Half Cross-Stitch

Advantages

Excellent for outlining and filling in shapes.

Very applicable for left-handers.

A fast stitch—about 15 minutes to work 1 square inch.

For working 1 square inch, I average 2 yards of single strands of wool, working with one strand doubled; 1 yard of triple strands.

Disadvantages

Can be used only on double, not on single mesh.

Pulls out of shape more easily than the other stitches.

Basket Weave (or Bias Tent)

Advantages

When working this stitch, the canvas is never turned around. ("Top" always remains at the top.)

The canvas holds its shape well.

Perfect for diagonal designs.

Excellent for large areas and backgrounds.

Most applicable for left-handers.

Good for both petit point and gros point.

Can be worked on both mono and penelope.

It takes about 20 minutes to work 1 square inch.

For working 1 square inch, I average 2½ yards of single strands of wool with single strand doubled, 1½ yards of a pair of strands not doubled.

After working 2 pairs of strands, where 1 strand in each case has been discarded from the original 3, the 2 discarded make another pair.

16
Summing up on Stitches

The time element noted to cover a square inch is deliberately geared at a relaxed pace, not aimed at a contest pitch.

Some prefer to do all their needlepoint in basket weave because it keeps the canvas in shape. I recommend it only to the very experienced, because it takes skill to fill in irregular shapes with the basket weave. However, most prefer to work the *shapes* in Continental and the *large areas* or *background* in basket weave.

To gauge the exact amount of yarn needed is impossible. Everyone varies in the amount he uses, but approximate amounts are given at the end of the book (chapter 56).

Make your stitches *puffy*. This will help keep the canvas from being pulled out of line.

Never use a length of wool, whether doubled or single, longer than 18 inches for needlepoint or 12 inches for petit point.

Before pulling the yarn through the canvas, always hold the yarn flush with the canvas (Fig. 3f). This keeps it from bunching at the needle's point of entry. If using the needle up and down in two motions, hold the yarn taut underneath the canvas in the same way as the needle comes up.

17
Left-Handed Needlepoint

Left-handed needlepoint has its handicaps. Being left-handed myself I am aware of them. Obviously invented by a right-handed person, needlepoint is geared to what is natural to him. I see no reason for the stitches not to slant like the accent grave [\] as opposed to the accent acute [/], but I suppose in competition this might be looked down on by unimaginative judges.

After you read the directions for right-handed needlepoint and become familiar with the direction of the three stitches, begin with the Continental. The canvas is worked in *exactly* the same direction as the right-hander would do it. Shapes and objects take priority at the upper right of the real top and from there stitches will travel down to the lower left.

By interpreting directions for the right-handed, the left-hander should be able to follow any book and not be isolated by his own separate rules.

REMEMBER, any mention of TOP means the REAL TOP, which in your case will vary from being on the right or left. Don't forget that in the penelope canvas the close-together threads are *parallel* to the sides and so will always be horizontal to the left-hander.

Left-Handed Continental

After you have taped your square of canvas, write TOP on the tape, on an edge at right angles to the selvage.

Turn back to Figure 6 and turn the book counterclockwise so that encircled numbers will be facing you. As you begin you will be holding the book and the canvas with the true TOP of the book at the left (designated by arrows), and you will be following NUMBERS rather than LETTERS.

1. Begin at the upper left-hand corner UP, DOWN, UP, encompassing the corner lines of your square (Fig. 6, 1).
2. Proceed down the canvas toward yourself (Fig. 6, 2).
3. DOWN on the 10th stitch (Fig. 6, 3).
4. Turn the canvas (but not the book) so that TOP is now at your RIGHT. Bring the needle UP (Fig. 6, 4).
5. Again work down the canvas toward yourself, with the real TOP and all even rows on your RIGHT (Fig. 6, 5).
6. DOWN on the 10th stitch of the row (Fig. 7, 6).
7. Turn canvas so TOP is at LEFT. Bring the needle UP (Fig. 7, 7).
8. Again work DOWN toward yourself (Fig. 7, 8).
9. Continue in this manner through the 10th row, UP, DOWN on the last hole (Fig. 7, 9). Slip your yarn under a few stitches and clip.

For the *ambidextrous* the Continental can avoid superfluous motion and be very swift if you work from right to left with the right hand

and then left to right with the left hand. This left-to-right stitch will be referred to as the AMBI-D stitch.

For the left-hander a piece could be worked completely in the AMBI-D stitch (Fig. 14). In this case the rules would be the opposite of those for the Continental right-hander.

Song of the AMBI-D

You may be a SOUTHpaw from the WEST
But NORTH and EAST you travel best.
For you it is UP and for you it is RIGHT
Remember this rule and never lose sight:
Always go UP and always go RIGHT.

Left-Handed Basket Weave

Turn back to Figure 8. Again turn the book ¼ counterclockwise, keeping the real TOP of the canvas continually at your left (see Figs. 8, 9). All directions in complete reverse of, and at right angles to right-handed ones are italicized.

1. UP, DOWN, UP, with the 1st stitch encompassing an intersection of the canvas where the *vertical* thread is uppermost, if you are using mono canvas (Fig. 8, 1). Keep true TOP of canvas at LEFT. (Remember in penelope canvas the close-together threads are *parallel* to the sides.)

2. On the 2nd DOWN stitch, position your needle *horizontally,* going under stitch 1 as you complete another stitch at the real TOP and start a 2nd on the *right* of stitch 1 (Fig. 8, 2).

3. Complete the 2nd stitch and start the 3rd in a row that prepares you for the 2nd diagonal sequence of stitches (Fig. 8, 3).

4. In completing the 3rd stitch, position your needle *vertically* preparatory to working diagonally *down* the canvas to the left (Fig. 8, 4).

5. At the real TOP, complete the diagonal and start the 4th stitch *toward you,* UP, DOWN, positioning the needle *horizontally* for the next diagonal row *up* the canvas (Fig. 8, 5).

6. Complete the 4th stitch. Start the 5th, UP, DOWN, positioning the needle *vertically* preparatory to working diagonally *down* the canvas (Fig. 8, 6). Complete the diagonal. Continue in this manner with the needle in *horizontal* position working *up* and in *vertical* working *down* the canvas.

7. In completing the square the last "row" will consist of 1 stitch UP, DOWN. Slip your yarn under a few stitches and clip (Fig. 9, 7).

Left-Handed Half Cross-Stitch

Since this stitch goes from left to right, it will suit you very well. It's a natural for the left-hander; it seems awkward any other way.

Follow Figure 11, turning the canvas upside down at the end of the first row and working back. The canvas will be right side up every odd row.

To sum up the left-handed Continental: As you will see in Figure 6, when you are making a *solid* square the canvas is turned so that TOP alternates from left to right and you will be continually working DOWN the canvas (toward you).

Study the following diagram to see what happens when you make the *outline* of a square. The darkest arrows within the squares designate the immediate row you are working on and the pale arrows designate the row already worked.

The arrowheads outside the squares mark the real TOP. Be sure that TOP on your canvas tallies with TOP in the diagram and end each row with the needle DOWN (through the back side of the canvas) before changing direction.

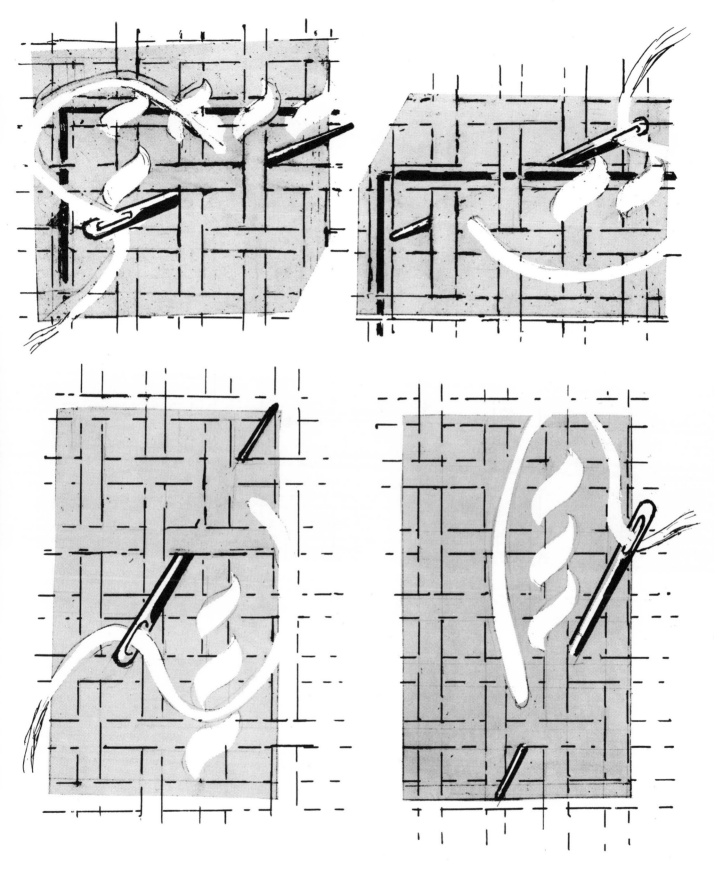

Fig. 14   The AMBI-D stitch   The Continental

As long as the stitches slant NE to SW in relationship to the true TOP, you are making legitimate needlepoint, and eventually you may invent your own way of holding the canvas. Experiment by working many small squares (solid and outline) on a fresh canvas. Remember, the selvage is always on the side. In penelope canvas the closest threads are vertical in relation to the top.

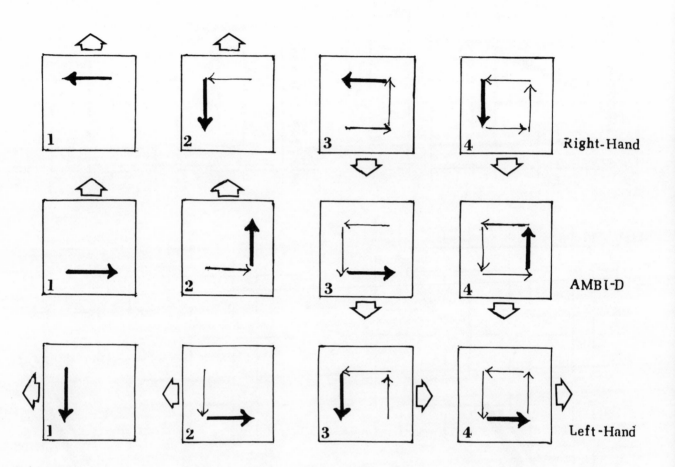

18
From Rabbits to Rectangles

Ventures in planning your design are fun. Naturally it is wise to pursue the subject matter that appeals to you. Just because there are so many bad floral and animal designs doesn't mean that they are all taboo.

Shown here, for example, are four rabbits, a COPTIC rabbit, a rabbit from an eighteenth-century chair seat, a CHINA rabbit, and a REALISTIC rabbit (Plates VI, VII, VIII, IX). The Copts, ancient Egyptians, were masters of design (Photograph 2, Graph 9). The background is as much of a shape as the subject. The background is very important. It has to integrate with the subject matter in such a way as to cause tension and rhythm.

In Rabbit from an Eighteenth-Century Chair, a striped background has been introduced (2nd animal on Graph 10).

In the case of the REALISTIC rabbit (Graph 11), which was traced over a photograph onto graph paper, the opposite is true. The background is kept white like most of the rabbit so as not to call attention to it. For instance, if the rabbit is gray and white and the background is brilliant orange, one would become aware of a very uninteresting shape.

In the case of the CHINA rabbit (Graph 12) the background shape is a little more interesting than the realistic rabbit but not enough to have it too much of a contrast.

The CAROUSEL rabbit (Graph 13, Plates Xa and Xb) should have a background that is not too contrasting. Otherwise it would swamp the delicacy of the design.

So from rabbits to geometrics, it's important to think of the flow from foreground to background.

Geometrics can often create great illusions of depth, like the traditional Greek key design (Graph 14), and the lines leading from one "key" to the other look like rectangles in perspective.

Photograph 2 Coptic Rabbit. Medallion, Coptic, Fourth to Seventh Century A.D. *Courtesy, Museum of Fine Arts, Boston, Ross Collection* (Graph 9, Plate VI)

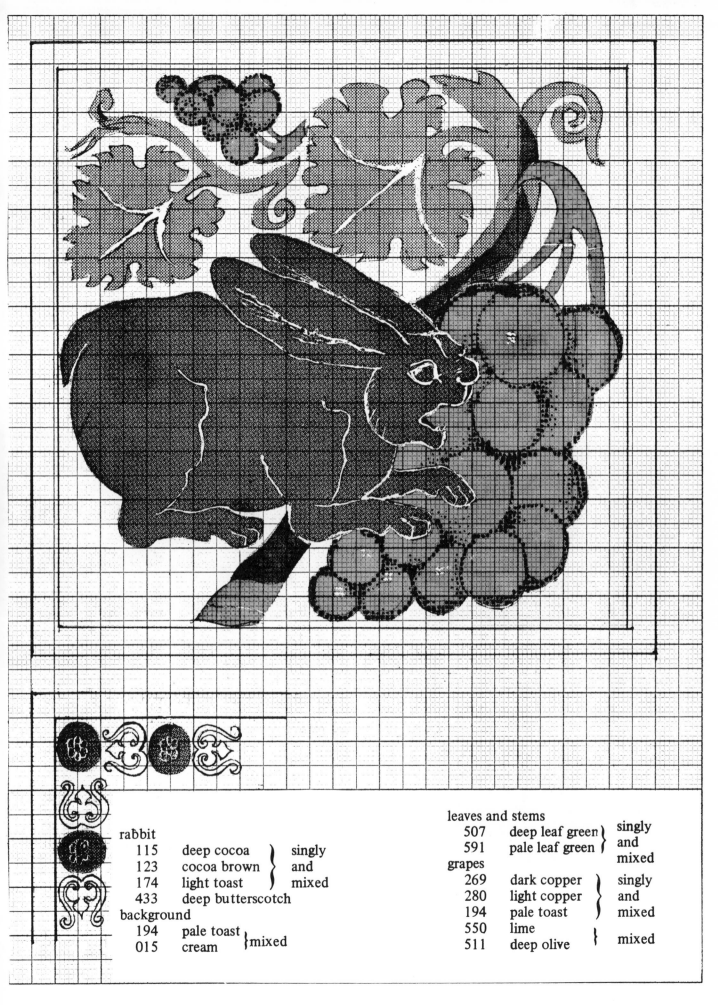

rabbit
    115   deep cocoa   } singly
    123   cocoa brown } and
    174   light toast   } mixed
    433   deep butterscotch
background
    194   pale toast } mixed
    015   cream

leaves and stems
    507   deep leaf green } singly
    591   pale leaf green } and mixed
grapes
    269   dark copper } singly
    280   light copper } and
    194   pale toast } mixed
    550   lime
    511   deep olive } mixed

Graph 9 Coptic Rabbit on #20 graph (Photograph 2,
Plate VI)

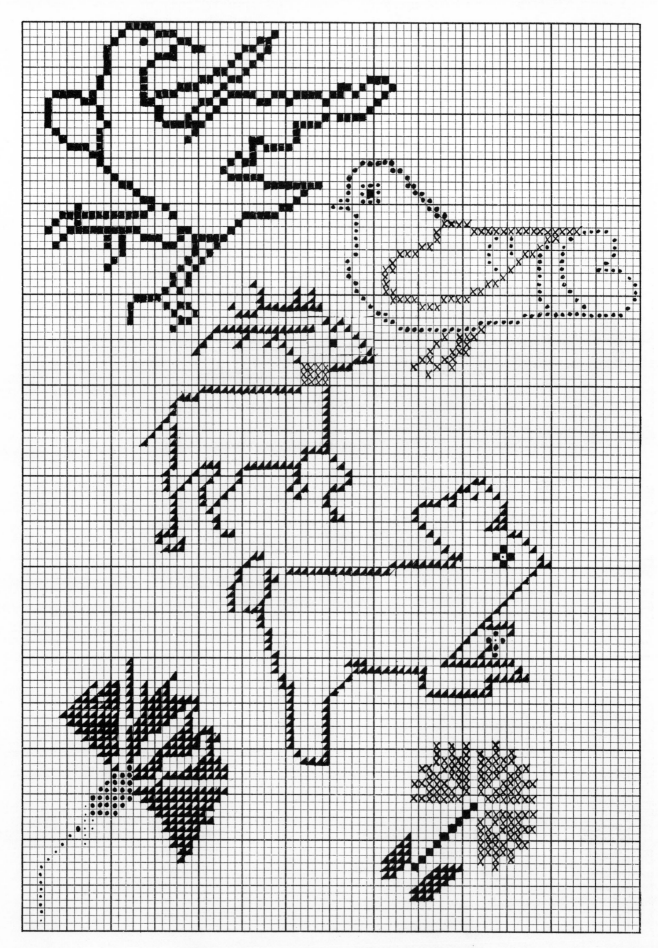

64

Graph 10 Animals, birds, and flowers on #12 graph.
Adaptations from samplers at the Metropolitan Museum of Art (animals and birds) and *American Samplers* by Bolton and Coe, Dover Publications (flowers)

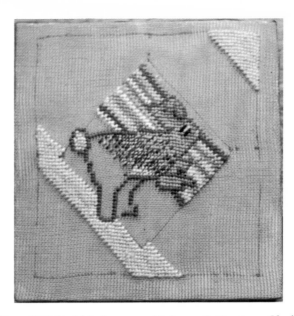

Plate VI Coptic Rabbit. 7½ x 7½ in. on #14 canvas (Graph 9, Photograph 2.)

Plate VII Rabbit from an Eighteenth-Century Chair. 7 x 7 in. on #12 canvas (Graph 10)

Plate VIII Realistic Rabbit. 6 x 8 in. on #12 canvas. Worked by Betsy Wiederhold (Graph 11)

Plate IX Chelsea China Rabbit. 8 x 12 in. on #10/20 canvas. Worked by Betsy Wiederhold (Graph 12)

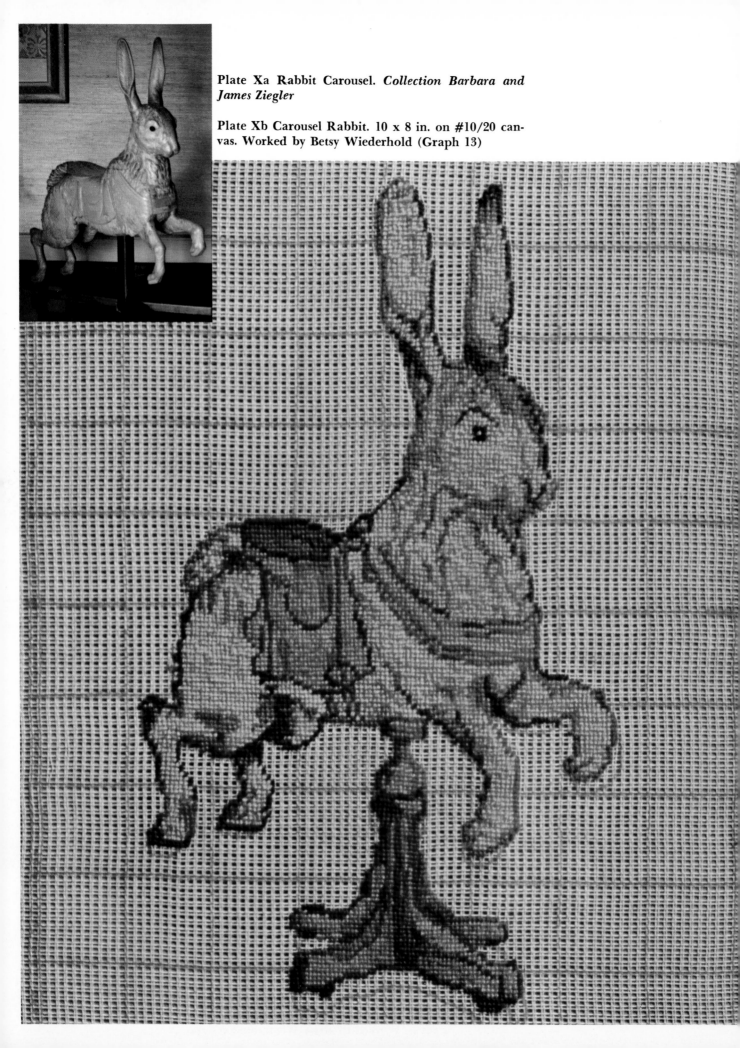

Plate Xa Rabbit Carousel. *Collection Barbara and James Ziegler*

Plate Xb Carousel Rabbit. 10 x 8 in. on #10/20 canvas. Worked by Betsy Wiederhold (Graph 13)

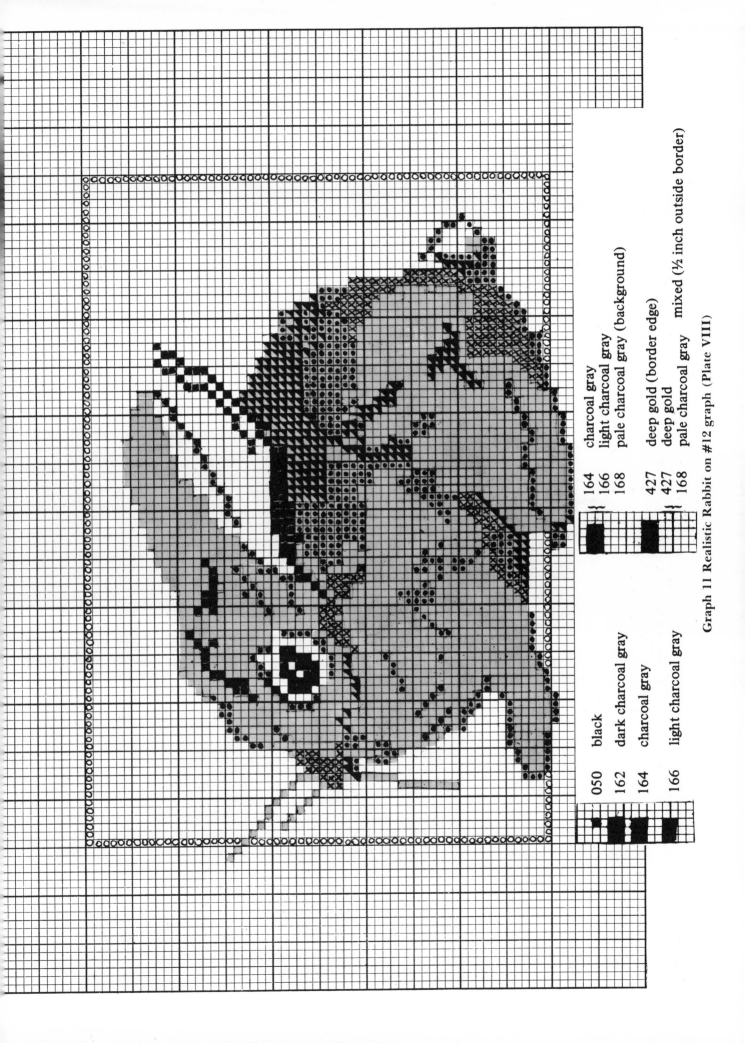

050　　black

162　　dark charcoal gray

164　　charcoal gray

166　　light charcoal gray

164 ⎤
166 ⎦　　{ charcoal gray
166 　　 light charcoal gray
168 　　 pale charcoal gray (background)

427 ⎤
427 ⎦　　{ deep gold (border edge)
　　 deep gold
168 　　 pale charcoal gray　　mixed (½ inch outside border)

Graph 11 Realistic Rabbit on #12 graph (Plate VIII)

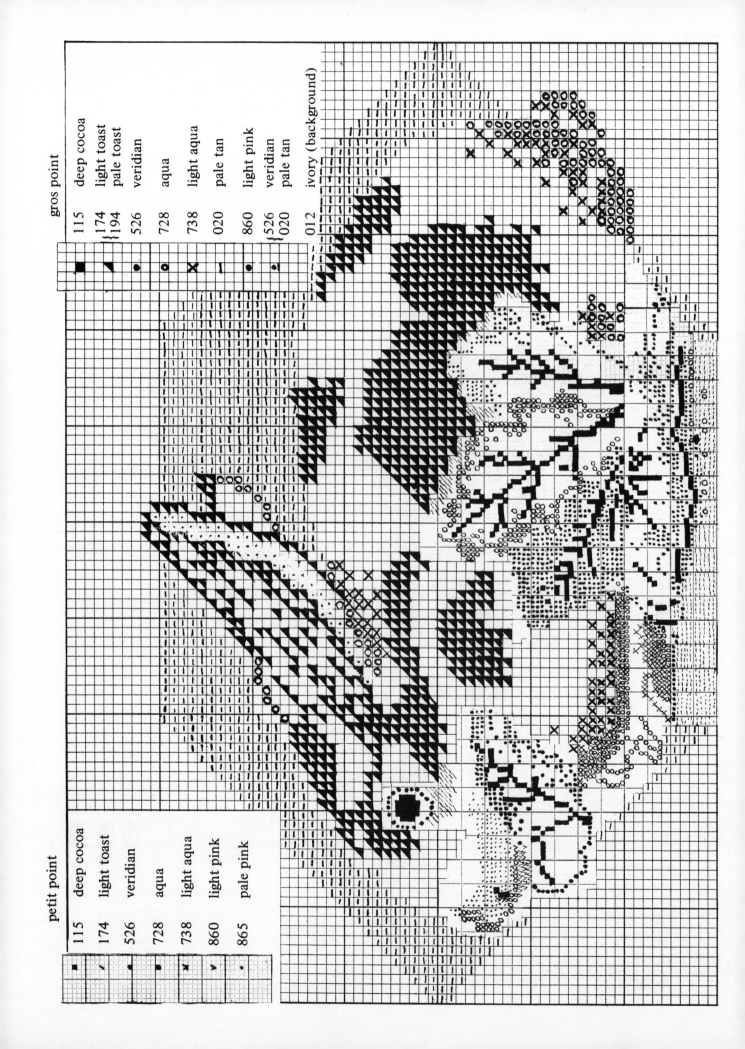

gros point

115	deep cocoa	■
174	light toast	◣
194	pale toast	
526	veridian	●
728	aqua	◉
738	light aqua	✕
020	pale tan	I
860	light pink	●
526	veridian	●
020	pale tan	
012	ivory (background)	

petit point

115	deep cocoa	■
174	light toast	╱
526	veridian	●
728	aqua	●
738	light aqua	✕
860	light pink	﹀
865	pale pink	·

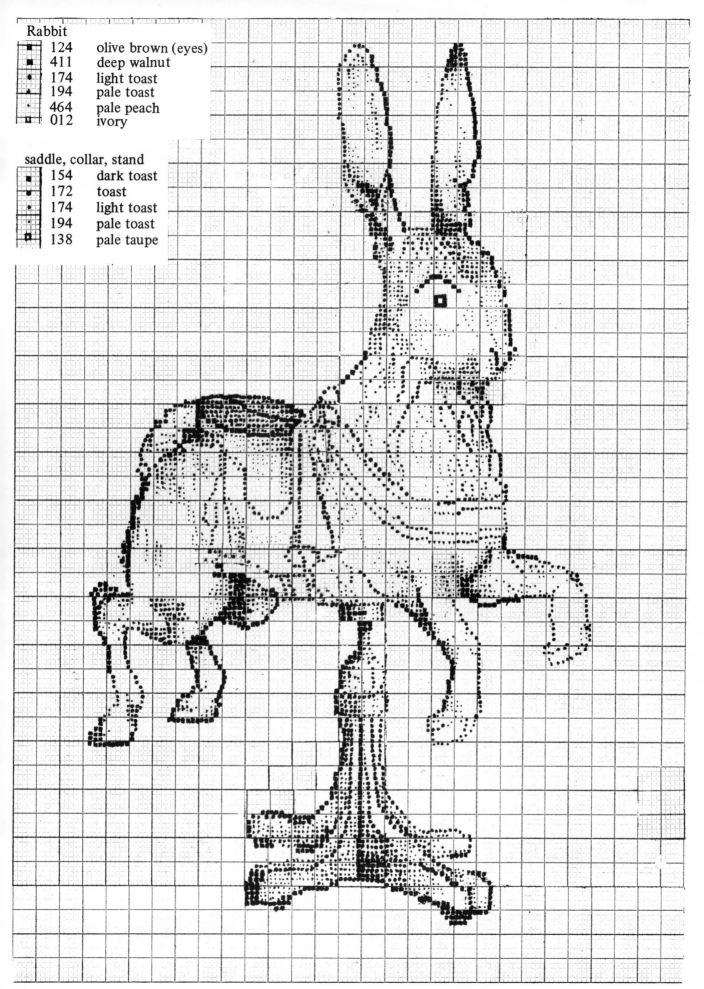

Rabbit

■	124	olive brown (eyes)
■	411	deep walnut
•	174	light toast
▲	194	pale toast
·	464	pale peach
□	012	ivory

saddle, collar, stand

■	154	dark toast
▲	172	toast
•	174	light toast
·	194	pale toast
□	138	pale taupe

Graph 13 Carousel Rabbit on #20 graph (Plate Xb)
Adaptation of a Carousel (Plate Xa) *Collection of*
Barbara and James Ziegler

Graph 14 Borders on #20 graph. With the exception
of the traditional Greek key, the designs are from
the D.M.C. Encyclopedia

19
Poodles and Pussycats

At a needlepoint show the prize usually goes to a poodle or a Siamese cat. Even the staunchest animal lover, if he knows anything about good design, should deplore these trophy winners.

These thoroughbreds seem to mesmerize the jury with their needlepoint eyes! As an animal lover myself, I don't like to downgrade them, but it does seem as if pets and complicated stitchery go together.

It is absolutely imperative that you learn to stitch perfectly, but beyond that, the design should take priority over a display of an exercise in stitchery.

For example, an owl might be done in a fantastic combination of "plaited gobelin," "encroaching oblique," "herringbone," and "double leviathan," and integrated with great skill, and still be a very poor design. The sooner juries realize this, the sooner needlepoint designs will take a turn for the better.

"A good design is a matter of personal taste," people are apt to say.

But I think there are a few rules. An object of any kind against a background that has no relation to it, no flow between it and the rest of the canvas, no concern over the shape of the background as complementary to that of the subject, cannot be considered a good design.

Study Bottle and Glass (Photograph 3, Graph 15) and La Valse (Photograph 4, Graph detail 16), where background and foreground are so integrated that there is no sharp division between the two. In fact, I hope you feel that this rule applies to all the designs in this book.

Photograph 3 Bottle and Glass on Table. 1912–13, Ink and Pasted Paper, by Pablo Picasso. *The Metropolitan Museum of Art, The Alfred Stieglitz Collection, 1949* (Graph 15)

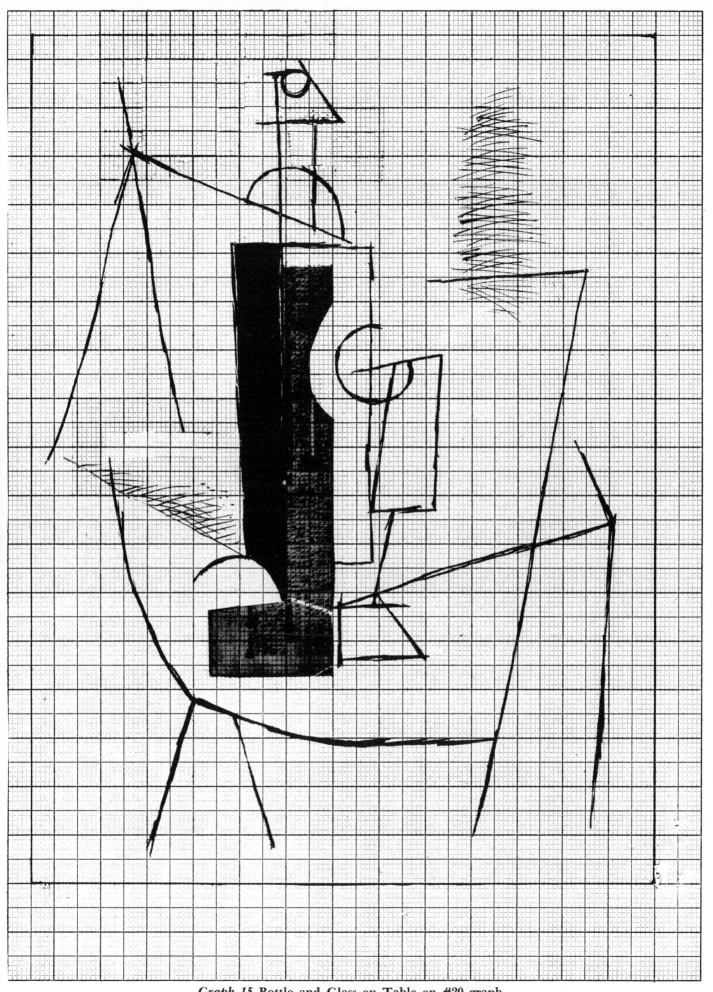

Graph 15 Bottle and Glass on Table on #20 graph.
Adaptation of a Collage by Pablo Picasso (Photograph 3)

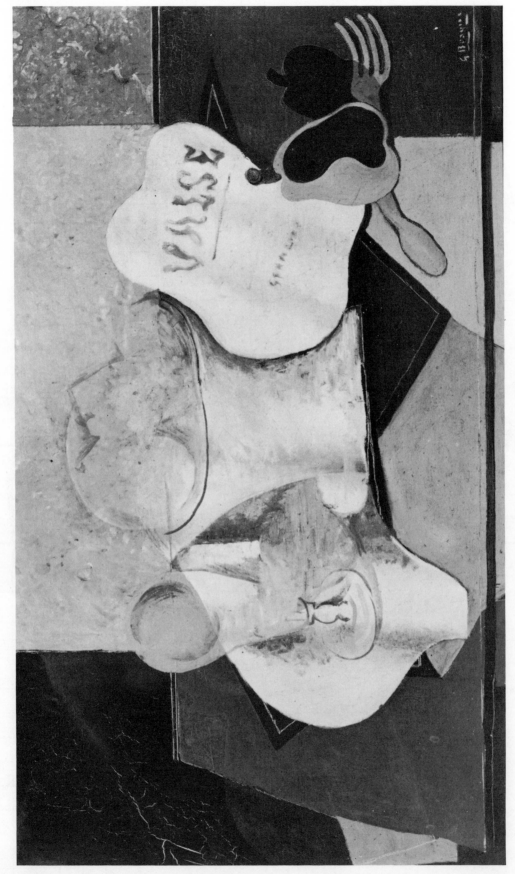

Photograph 4 La Valse (Still Life: Compote and Fruit). 1928, Georges Braque. *Philadelphia Museum of Art, The A. E. Gallatin Collection (Graph 16)*

050   black
352   pale spruce green (pear)-solidly and intermixed
136   light olive brown (table and sheet-music)-solidly and intermixed
513   pale dill (light areas and background)

Graph 16 La Valse, Still Life: Compote and Fruit on
#20 graph (detail). Adaptation from the painting by
Georges Braque (Photograph 4)

20
Patience

I wouldn't have the patience." How many times has this phrase been said! Patience pays off.

After a grueling experience in carrying out a complicated design, there is *such* a wonderful feeling of accomplishment, and sometimes there is a dividend, like a simple idea that turns into a pattern easy to do—fun and effective.

21
Respect for the Square!

Knowing that needlepoint is made up of squares and featuring this will eliminate a lot of disappointments. Petit point is usually anywhere from 16 to 24 mesh to the inch, or 16 to 24 point canvas. Anything less is gros point.

When shops exhibit painted needlepoint canvases of curved fruits and flowers on 10 point, they are not giving a true picture of what is going to happen when the design is worked.

Nevertheless, a rose doesn't *have* to be rounded. Graph 39 (on #10 graph) and Graph 40 (on #16 graph) simply give different effects. But it's important to know the effect you are going to get before you start.

It takes considerable planning to make a smoothly rounded rose into a graph design.

A lot of practice on graph paper making your designs fit into squares not only is great fun but, as you pursue this practice, more and more ideas will present themselves.

When you are advanced in needlepoint proficiency, try these two charming rose textiles (Photographs 5, 6, Graphs 17, 18) from the Metropolitan. Be sure that the roses and backgrounds keep to the same shades and tones so that the play between foreground and background is constant.

Photograph 5 Red Roses. German, Eighteenth Century. *The Metropolitan Museum of Art, Rogers Fund, 1909* (Graph 17)

Graph 17 Red Roses on #16 graph. Adaptation of a
German textile (Photograph 5)

Photograph 6 Brocade Roses in gray, black, and white. *The Metropolitan Museum of Art, Gift of the United Piece Dye Works* (Graph 18)

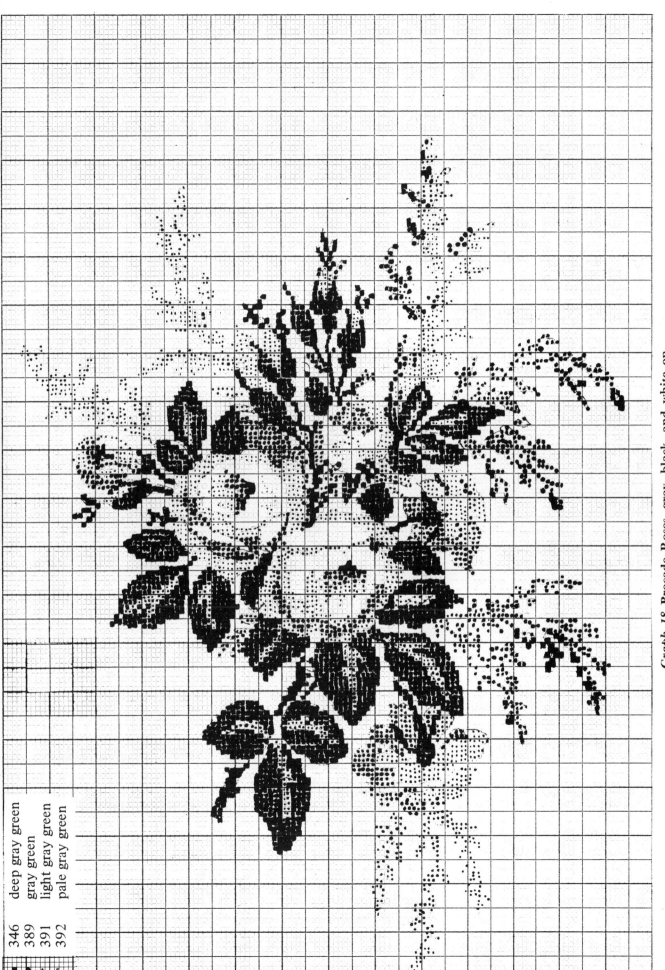

346   deep gray green
389   gray green
391   light gray green
392   pale gray green

Graph 18 Brocade Roses—gray, black, and white on #20 graph. Adaptation of a textile (Photograph 6)

22
Making the Circle

Depending on the size you want your circle to be and the gauge of your canvas or graph paper, you will find that different effects will occur. Different squares will be filled in each time to produce the roundest circle.

For example, a small circle on 10 point (10 squares to the inch) gauge canvas is not going to be so round as a large circle. In other words, the larger the circle and the more squares to the inch, the rounder the circle will be.

Study Figure 15 for the various effects of small and larger circles on graph paper from 10 to 20 squares to the inch. Figure 16 shows step-by-

step directions for filling in a solid circle, Figure 17 for outlining a circle, and Figure 18 and Photograph 7 for radiation of circles.

After you have become proficient with the circle, try variations. Angel and Dolphin (Photograph 8, Graph 19), with its uneven circle in the background, accentuates the old textile charm of the piece, whereas in Vine with Animals (Photograph 9, Graph 20) and Walking Bird (Photograph 10, Graph 21), the treatment of the leaves gives an illusion of a circle. Look for more variations of the circle throughout this book.

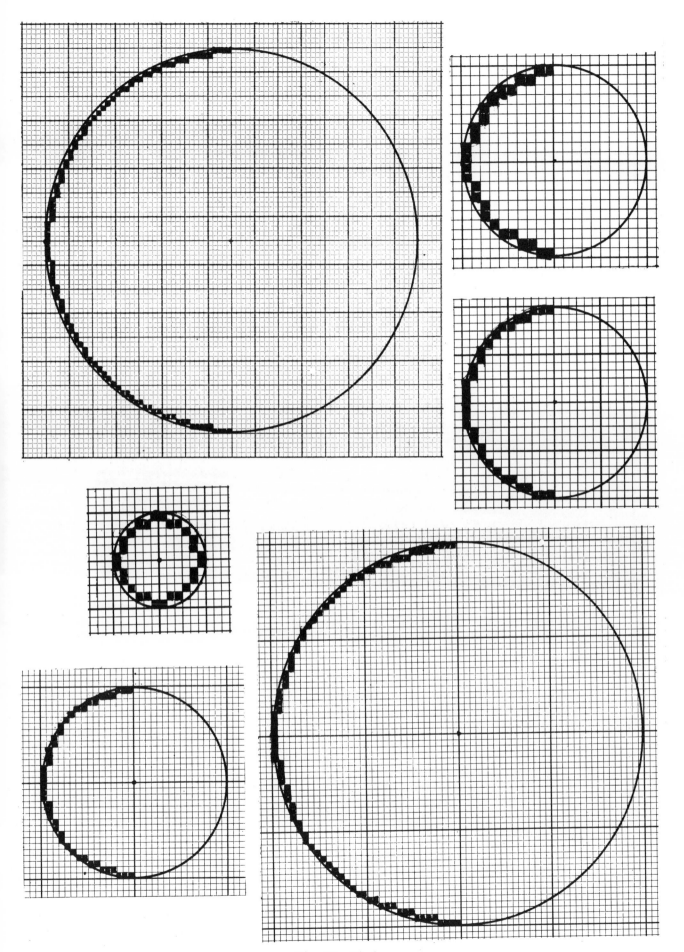

Fig. 15 Circles

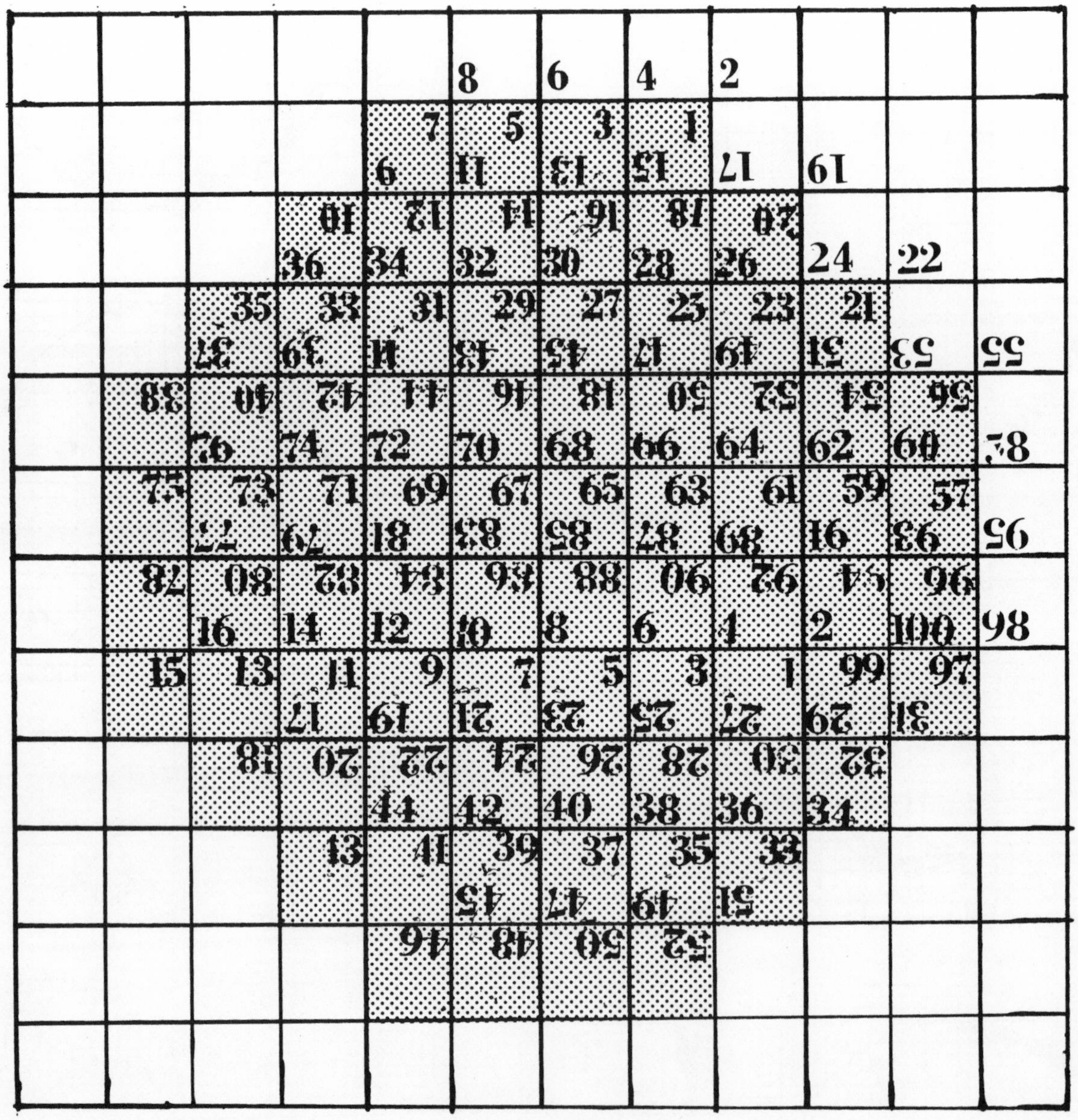

Fig. 16   A solid circle

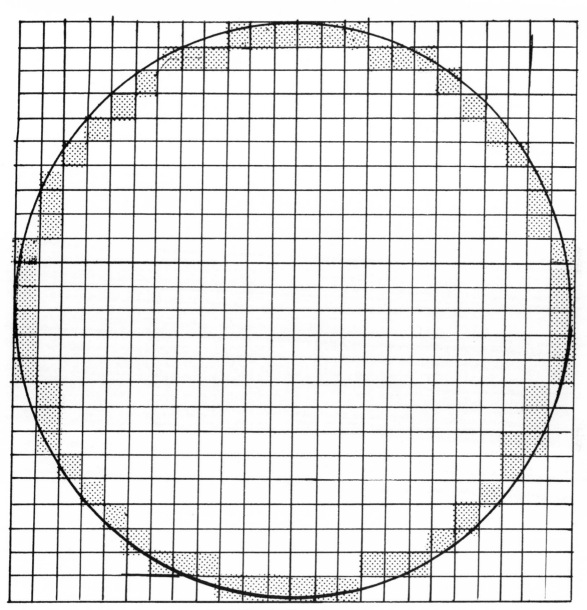

Fig. 17 Outline of a circle

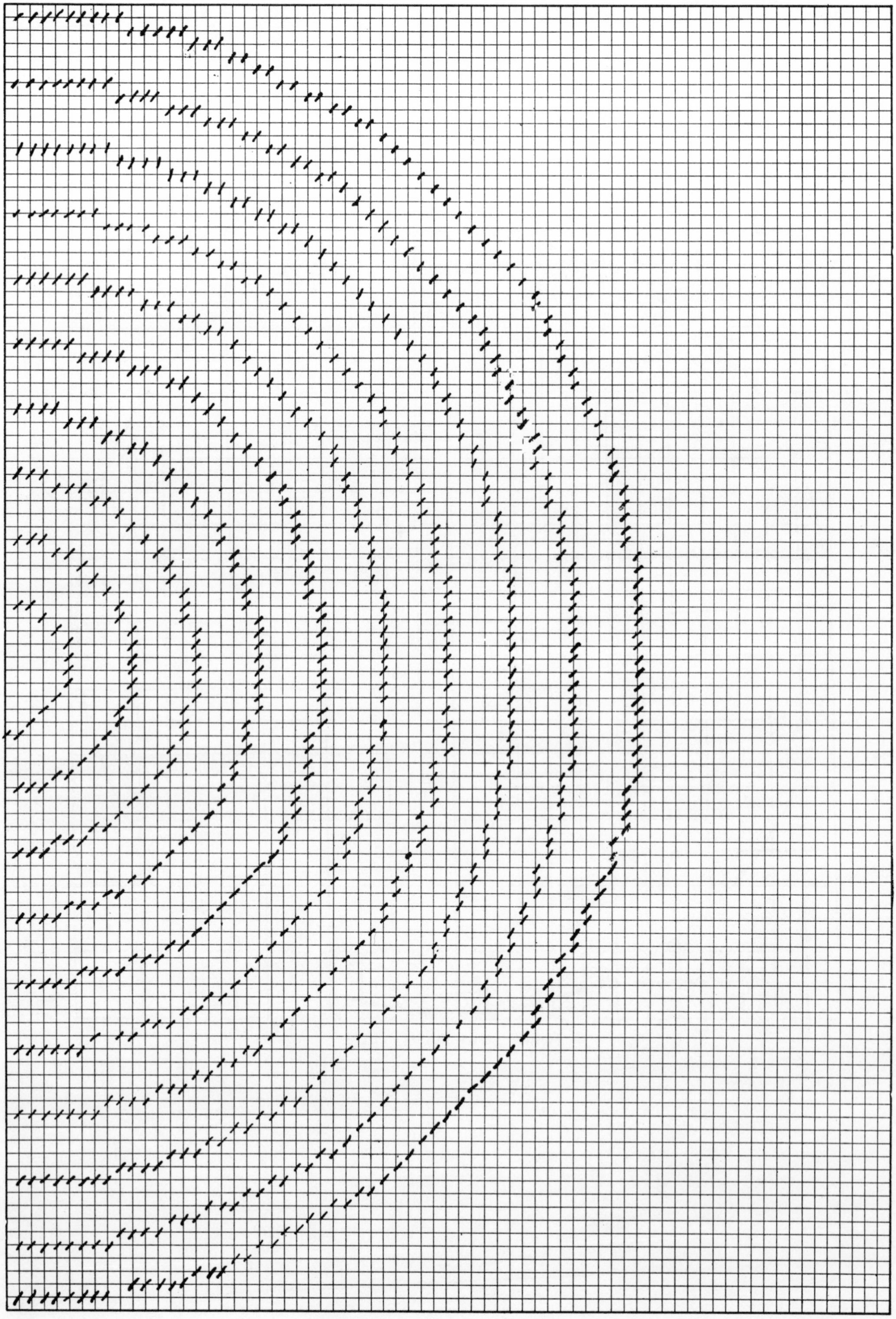

Fig. 18 Radiating circles

Photograph 7 Radiating Circles (Figure 18)

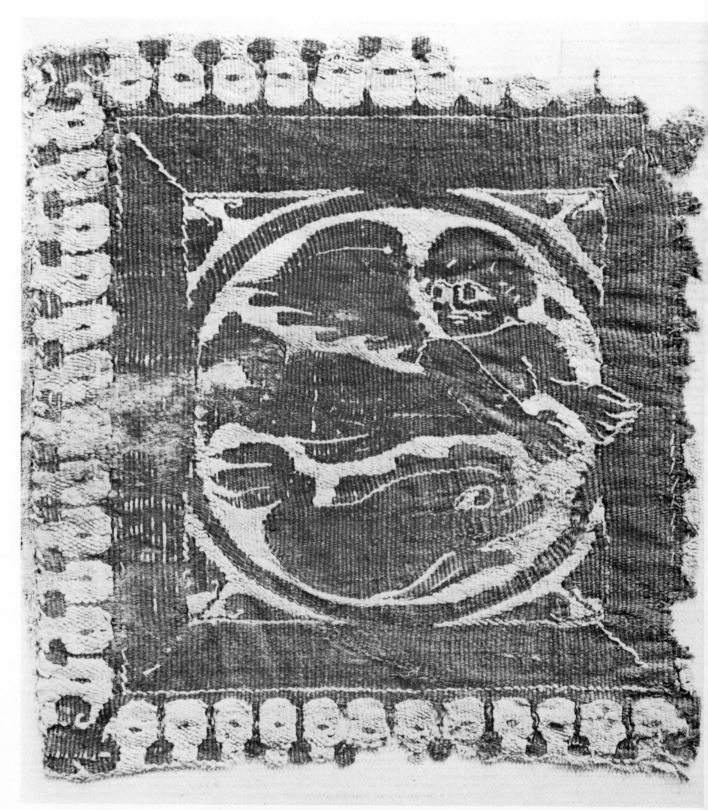

Photograph 8 Angel and Dolphin. Coptic, Sixth Century A.D. *The Brooklyn Museum, Gift of the Pratt Institute* (Graph 19)

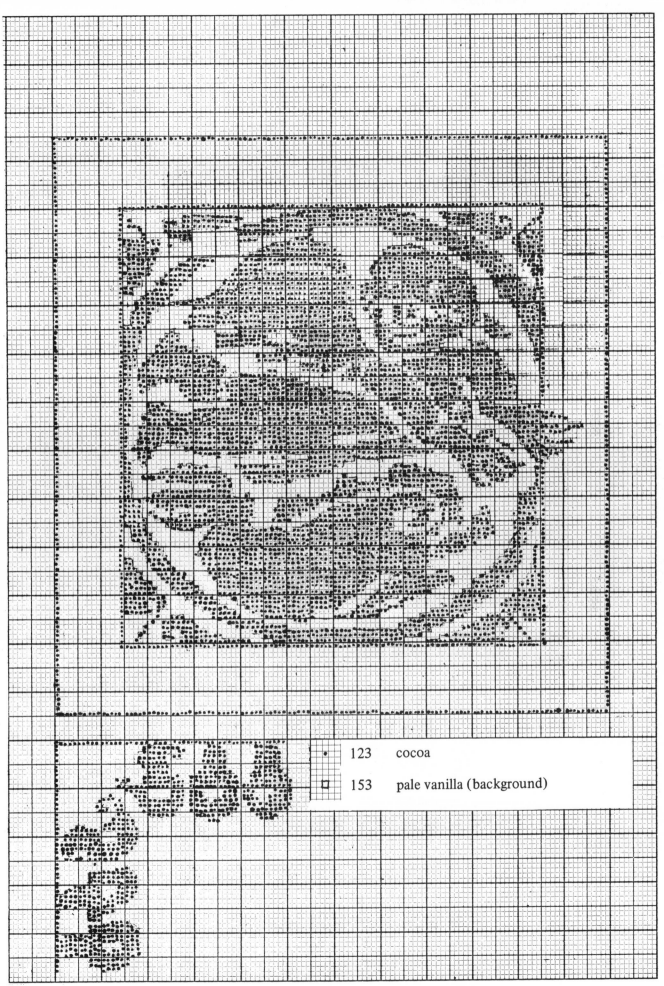

123 cocoa

153 pale vanilla (background)

Graph 19 Angel and Dolphin on #20 graph. Adaptation of a Coptic textile (Photograph 8)

Photograph 9 Vine with Animals. Coptic, Fourth to Fifth Century A.D. *The Brooklyn Museum, Gift of the Pratt Institute* (Graph 20)

| 308 | navy (trunk, leaves) | 579 | mint (border on vase) |
| 225 | venetian red (vase, rabbit and details) | 531 | light olive (background and line drawing on vase) |

Graph 20 Vines with Animals on #20 graph. Adaptation of a Coptic textile (Photograph 9)

Photograph 10 Walking Bird. Coptic Adaptation.
Staatliche Museen zu Berlin (Graph 21)

90

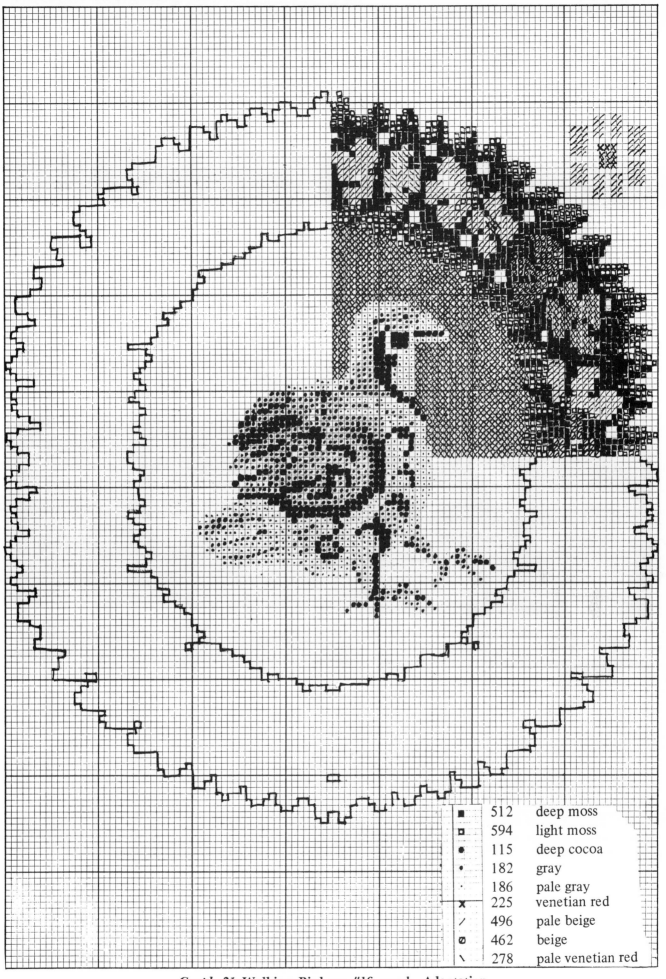

■	512	deep moss
▫	594	light moss
●	115	deep cocoa
•	182	gray
·	186	pale gray
✕	225	venetian red
/	496	pale beige
∅	462	beige
＼	278	pale venetian red

Graph 21 Walking Bird on #16 graph. Adaptation
from a Coptic textile (Photograph 10)

Photograph 11 The Blue Cat. Detail, Cat, "The Cas-
well Rug." *The Metropolitan Museum of Art, Gift of
Katherine Keyes, 1938, in memory of her father,
Homer Eaton Keyes* (Graph 22, Graph 23, detail)

92

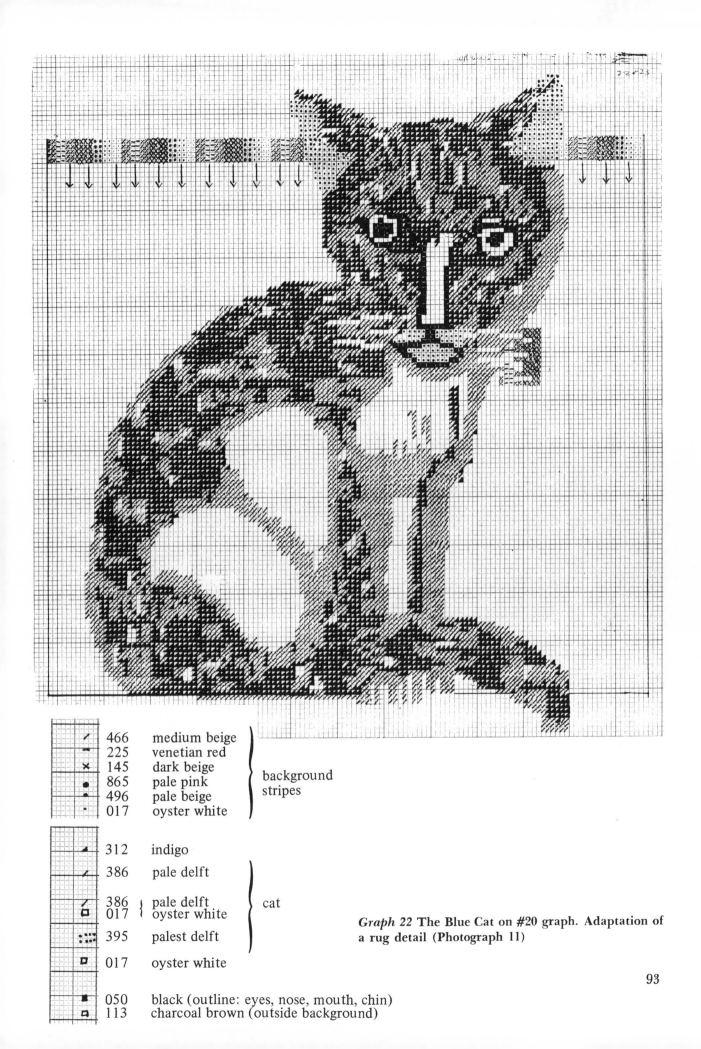

	466	medium beige	
	225	venetian red	
	145	dark beige	background
	865	pale pink	stripes
	496	pale beige	
	017	oyster white	
	312	indigo	
	386	pale delft	
	386	pale delft	cat
	017	oyster white	
	395	palest delft	
	017	oyster white	
	050	black (outline: eyes, nose, mouth, chin)	
	113	charcoal brown (outside background)	

Graph 22 **The Blue Cat on #20 graph. Adaptation of a rug detail (Photograph 11)**

93

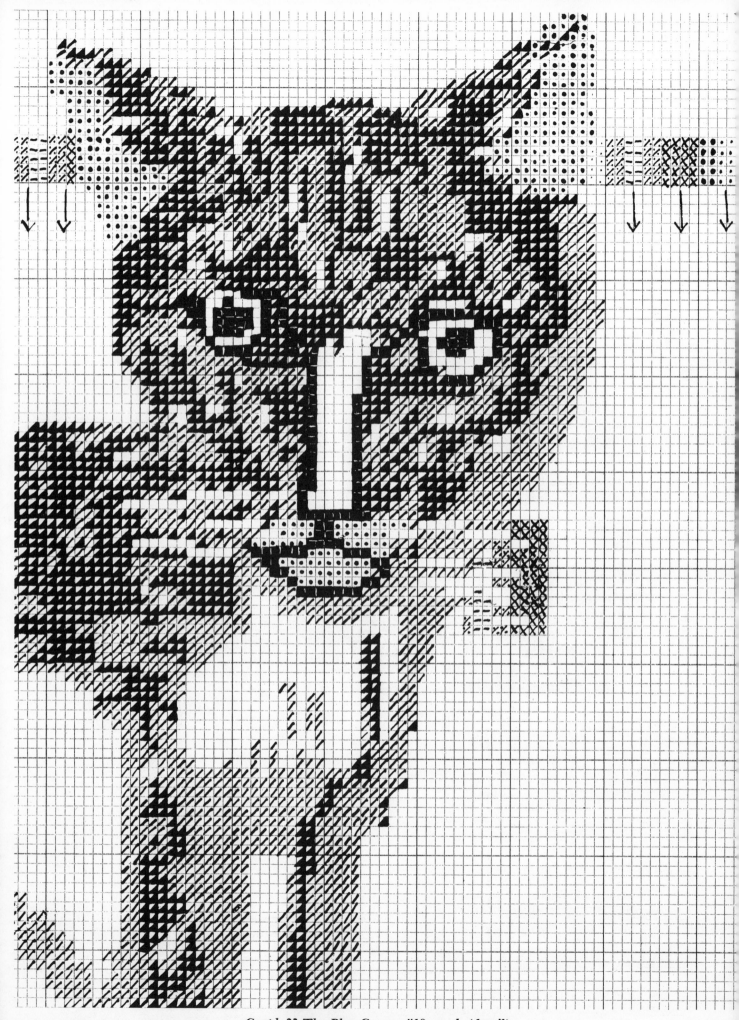

Graph 23 The Blue Cat on #10 graph (detail)

Photograph 12 Female Bust. Coptic, Eighth to Ninth Century A.D. *The Brooklyn Museum, Gift of the Pratt Institute* (Graph 24)

	308	navy (outside border, hair, eyebrows, eyes, nose, blouse edging)
	330	delft (oval border), hair, intermixed at random with navy)
	560	moss
	145	dark beige
	462	beige
	496	pale beige
	496	pale beige (eyes)
	234	copper rose

145 dark beige — singly and (face,
462 beige — intermixed blouse pattern,
496 pale beige — at random background)

Graph 24 Female Bust on #12 graph. Adaptation of
a Coptic textile (Photograph 12)

Plate XI Designs on canvas. By Betsy Borden

Plate XII Three first attempts. 3½ x 3½ in. on #12 canvas

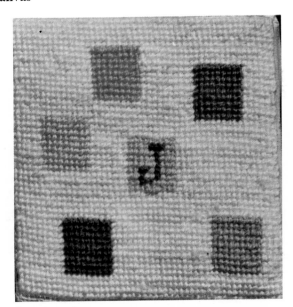

Plate XIII Three first attempts. 3½ x 3½ in. on #12 canvas

Plate XV "F." 3½ x 3½ in. on #14 canvas. Designed and worked by James Ziegler

Plate XIV Three first attempts. 3½ x 3½ in. on #5 canvas

Plate XVI Diamond. 3½ x 3½ in. on **#10** canvas

Plate XVII Diagonals. 3½ x 3½ in. on **#12** canvas

Plate XVIII Semicircles and Triangles. 3½ x 3½ in. on **#12** canvas

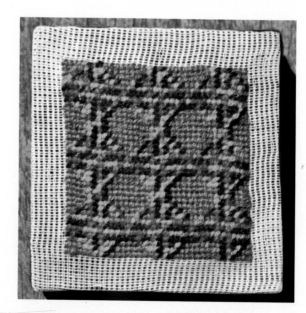

Plate XIX Caning. 3½ x 3½ in. on **#12** canvas (Graph 8)

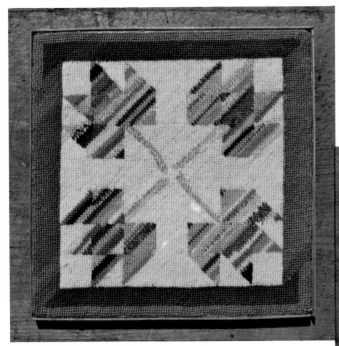

Plate XX Adaptation "Autumn Leaf," Early American Quilt. 12 x 12 in. on #10 canvas

Plate XXI Adaptation "Box" Pattern. 14 in. in diameter on #10 canvas. Designed by Ainsley and worked by Sue deWolf

Plate XXII Adaptation from Hatbox. 4½ x 4½ in. on #16 canvas

Plate XXIII Zinnia in progress. 14 in. in diameter on #12 canvas (Fig. 19)

23
You, Too, Can Be Creative

Many feel that being creative is out of reach—a miracle reserved for geniuses.

The greatest artists draw heavily on the art of the past, or some "crazy quilt" pattern of the present, or the arrangements of boats in a harbor, autumn leaves on a path, or spectators at a sports event.

For a more specific inspiration, my advice to needlepointers is, always carry a piece of graph paper in your pocket or bag. Who knows, you might find yourself at a dinner party about to sit on a petit point diningroom chair with a marvelous eighteenth-century rabbit that would make a perfect center for a pillow!

Always remember that being creative is spotting a great motif and making use of it. You don't even have to know how to draw. With your graph paper you simply count 2 up, 3 across, 1 up and 5 across, and so on. Go home with your treasure and work it into the center of a design. Notes on autumn leaves, for instance, could work out as a border, either as real leaves or as an abstract pattern.

Watch like a hawk for motifs you might work into your own design. At a museum, or in a book, or on rugs or tapestries you might find something that particularly appeals to you. Lift it out of its context and *use it*. Look at Photograph 11, Graph 22, a cat taken from a more involved early American rug design at the Metropolitan Museum. By itself it takes on a new dimension.

The well-known artist and teacher Stanley Hayter once said that there was one thing worse than being too influenced, and that was *not being influenced at all*. Hints of the past, of patterns in man-made art as well as nature, often make for more interesting subject matter than sheer originality.

Faces, unlike flowers, are seldom seen in needlepoint, so immediately here is a new impact. Study these three faces, Female Bust (Photograph 12, Graph 24), Head of Eros (Photograph 13, Graph 25), and the Face (Graphs 26, 27) as possibilities for a new look in needlepoint.

Photograph 13 Head of Eros. Coptic, Fourth Century A.D. *The Metropolitan Museum of Art, Gift of George D. Pratt* (Graph 25)

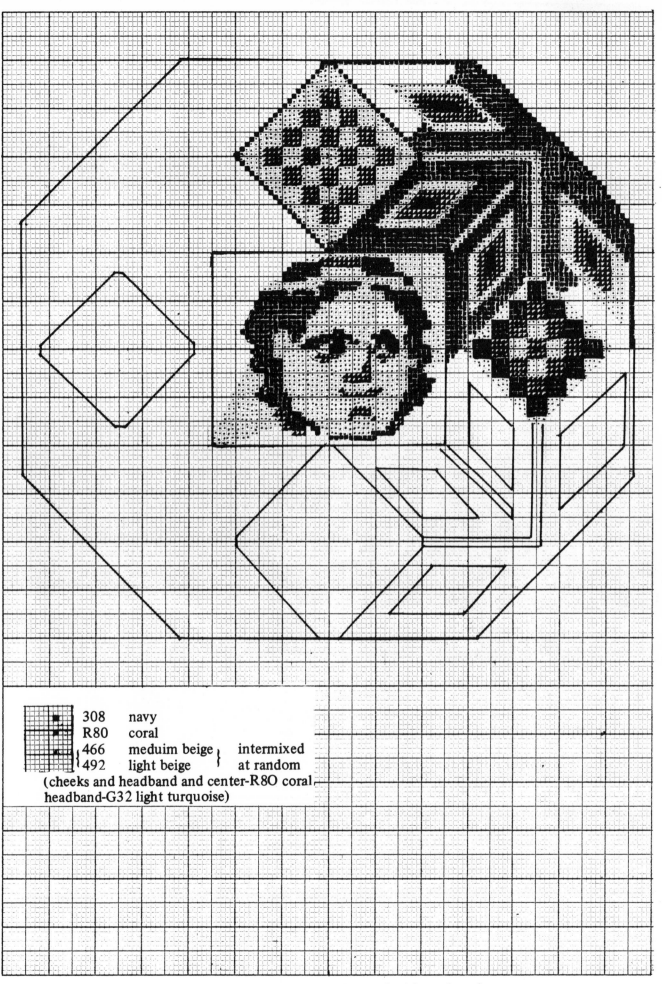

308   navy
R80   coral
{ 466   meduim beige }   intermixed
{ 492   light beige   }   at random
(cheeks and headband and center-R8O coral,
headband-G32 light turquoise)

Graph 25 Head of Eros on #20 graph. Adaptation of
a Coptic textile (Photograph 13)

	050	black	} intermixed
	610	deep woodviolet	at random (hair and blouse)
	137	light mauve (hair)	
	445	butterscotch	} intermixed
	440	mustard ochre	at random
	321	deep french blue	
	355	french blue	
	870	palest pink	

Graph 26 **The Face on #16 graph (detail). Adaptation of Tapisserie Copte. *Collection of Musée du Louvre***

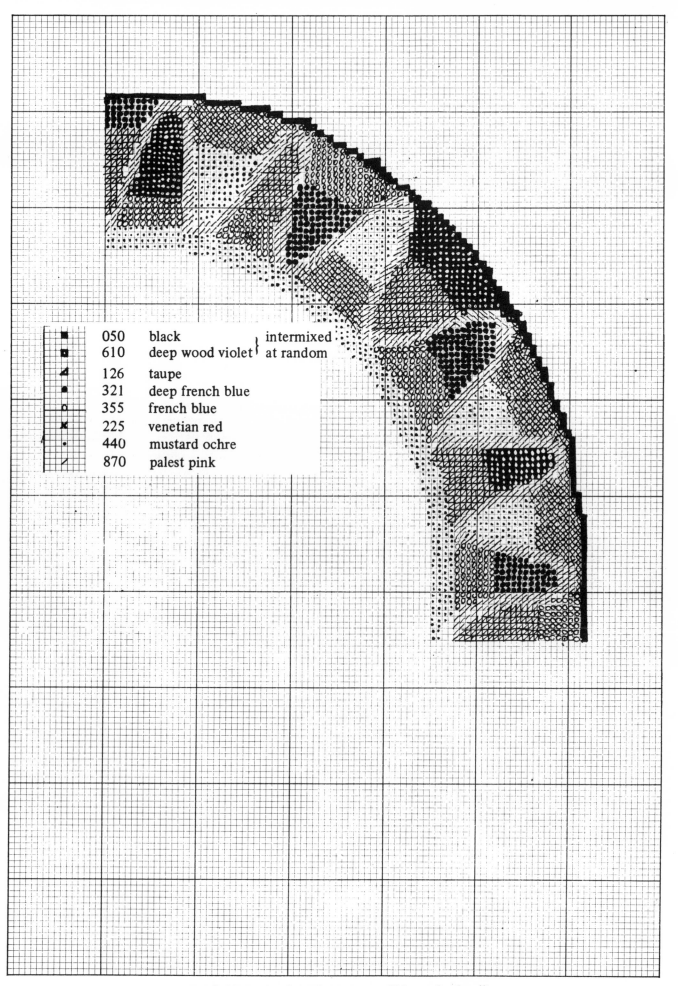

	050	black	intermixed
	610	deep wood violet	at random
	126	taupe	
	321	deep french blue	
	355	french blue	
	225	venetian red	
	440	mustard ochre	
	870	palest pink	

Graph 27 Border for The Face on #16 graph (detail)

24
Different Designs for Different Places

A small design like a coaster or a trivet or an eyeglass case can so conveniently be brought out of your bag for working at any leisure moment!

If you have a design where the subject matter requires concentration, do it when you are alone and leave the background to be worked at odd moments on the fly. Be sure to assemble your personal kit so it is ready to go along with you. Have you the right yarns, the right amount, your sketch, scissors, and proper needle? If you feel like stitching but haven't enough time or energy to assemble or to line up the equipment, you are wasting valuable moments.

The number of people whom I have seen idle at the airport, the station, the bus terminal, the doctor's and dentist's offices, the front porch, the beach, is appalling, when they could be having fun!

25
Motifs

Extend your vision! Always be on the lookout for motifs. Try to think for yourself. When you are driving keep your eyes open for designs—maybe a fence with scrolls; signs; building details. Cloud and rain effects can produce endless variations. Try to find things that are elastic in shape. There is a tendency to be too definite. Try to think of a *combination*. In a museum a Chinese vase might have a scene enclosed in an oval or rectangular space surrounded by a floral design. This might start your mind on your own scene or surroundings.

Keep away from a set design. Try to keep it fluid.

That is what is so wonderful about the Copts. They are never too hard and fast in their design. The background flows in and out and around the subject. (Look at Photographs 8, 9, 12, 13, 16.)

Museums

Museums can always produce an 8 x 10 photo of something you like, for a fee. For example, old musical instruments, Chinese vases, Early American art, animals, textiles, and other objects. In large cities most museums have textile departments that you can visit by procuring a permit. (See Photographs 10, 11, 13, 16.)

The subject matter is endless.

Here is an outline of some ideas to draw on for inspiration. See how many more you can add. Try to keep out of the owl and mushroom class, which has been overworked!

Nature

Flowers, trees, leaves, vines, branches, fruit

Animals

Cats, dogs, sheep, elephants, cows, horses, rabbits, birds. See Reclining Lamb (Photograph 14, Graph 28), Crouching Rabbit (Photograph 15, Graph 29), and Parrot (Photograph 16, Graph 30).

Insects

Butterflies, beetles, caterpillars

Changing Shapes and Effects in Nature

Sunlight, shadows, clouds, the ocean

Figures

Figures on Grecian urns, faces in early textiles

Architecture

Your own house, early New England farmhouse, Southern mansion, modern "A" frame, town hall, churches, town houses

Furniture

Tables (Photograph 17, Graph 32), chairs (Graph 33), vases, mirrors

Furniture is almost never seen in needlepoint, I suppose because needlepoint is usually considered furniture, but why not attempt this fresh field?

Small Objects

Playing cards (hearts, clubs, spades, and diamonds) (see Photograph 18 and Graphs 34, 35), chessmen, dice, fleur de lis, scrolls, plates, teapots, musical instruments

Plates are particularly successful in needlepoint because of their shape, but it might be interesting to try unusual objects. Why not try to do an antique teapot?

Photograph 14 Crewelwork, Eighteenth Century. *The Metropolitan Museum of Art, Collection of Mrs. Lathrop Colgate Harper, Bequest, 1957* (Graph 28)

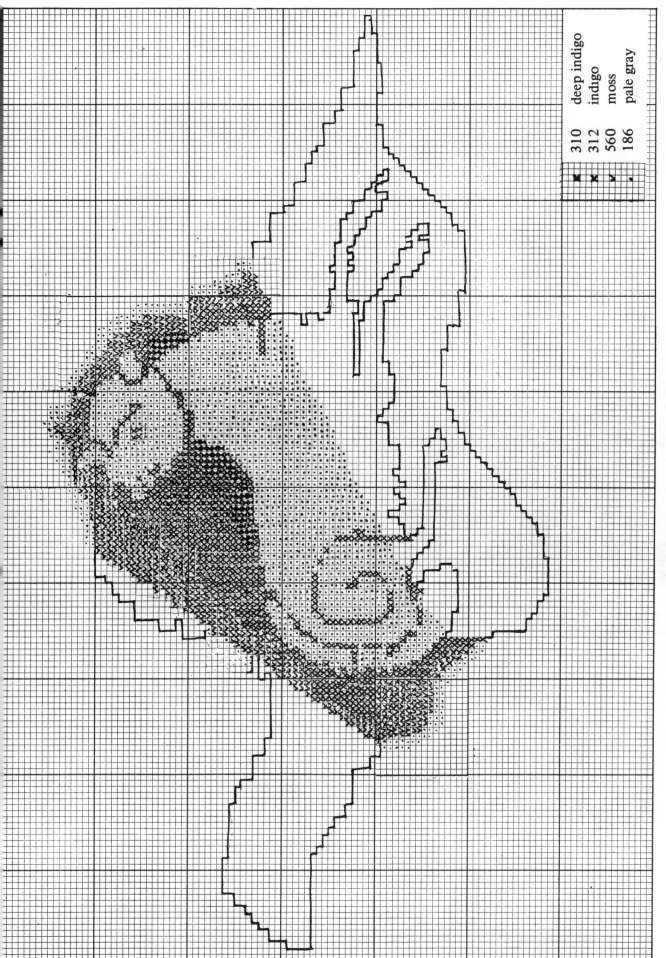

Graph 28 Reclining Lamb on #16 graph (detail).
Adaptation of a crewelwork (Photograph 14)

310	✖	deep indigo
312	✕	indigo
560	➤	moss
186	⋅	pale gray

Photograph 15 Textile, German, Nineteenth Century.
*The Metropolitan Museum of Art, Purchase 1901,
Rogers Fund* (Graph 29)

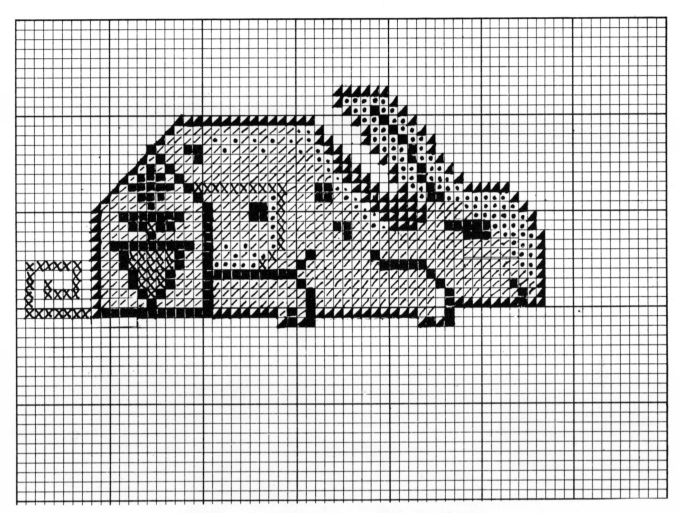

Graph 29 **Crouching Rabbit on #10 graph (detail).**
Adaptation of a German textile (Photograph 15)

Geometrics

Flowers, plants, and other examples of nature simplified into geometric designs

Patterns, Textiles, Paintings

Quilt designs, allover textiles, floor mosaics Autumn Leaf, Plate XX, shows how very simple quilt patterns can be elaborated on. To this effective geometric shape I have added diagonal stripes in the basket-weave stitch.

The traditional allover box pattern design, Plate XXI, reaches a new effect by confining it to a towering shape.

The hatbox, Plate XXII, is still another example of lifting a motif from a textile or wallpaper design.

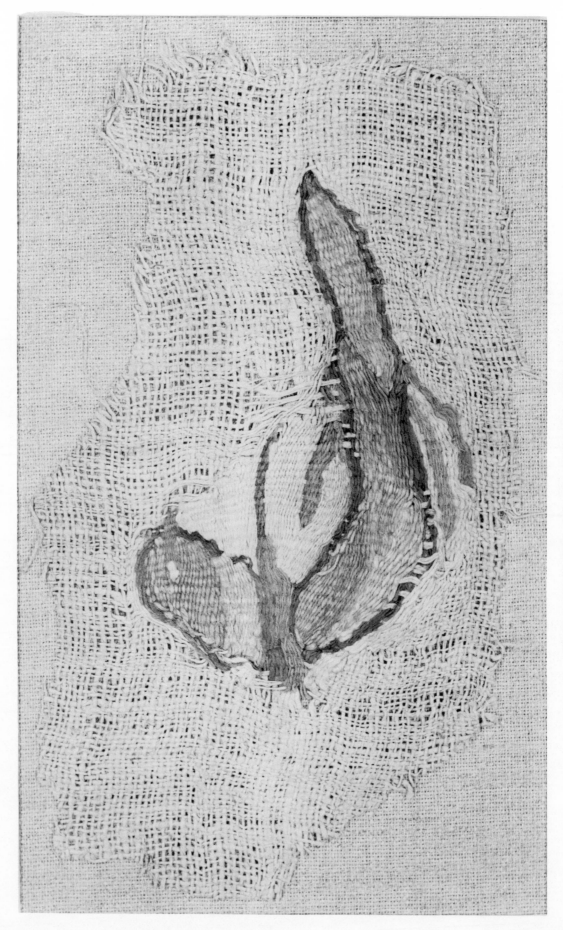

Photograph 16 Parrot. Coptic, Fifth to Sixth Century A.D. The Brooklyn Museum, Gift of the Pratt Institute (Graph 30)

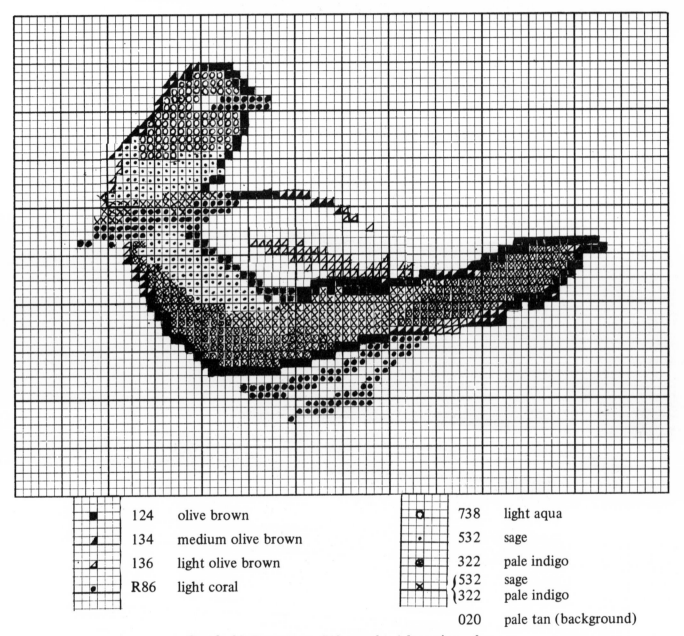

	124	olive brown		738	light aqua
	134	medium olive brown		532	sage
	136	light olive brown		322	pale indigo
	R86	light coral		532	sage
				322	pale indigo
				020	pale tan (background)

Graph 30 **Parrot on #12 graph. Adaptation of a Coptic textile (Photograph 16)**

Graph 31 Poésie de Mots on #20 graph. Adaptation from the etching by Jean Metzinger. *Collection of the author*

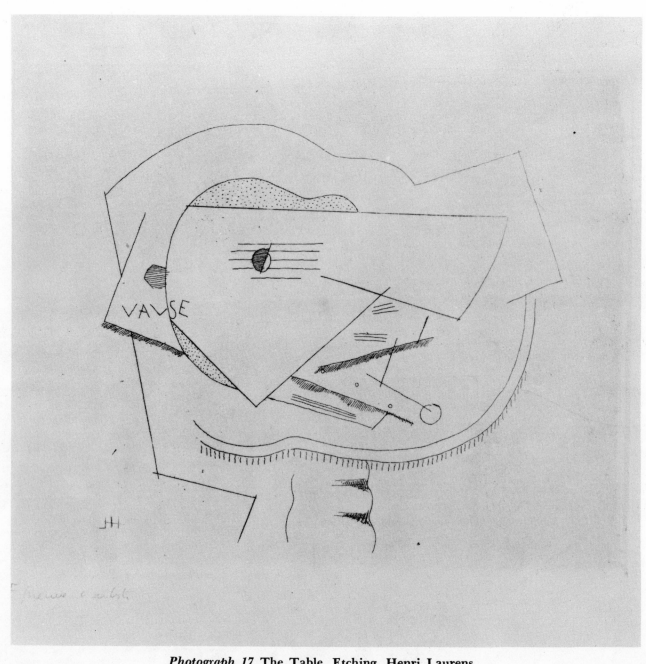

Photograph 17 **The Table. Etching, Henri Laurens, 1921.** *Galerie Louise Leiris, Paris* **(Graph 32)**

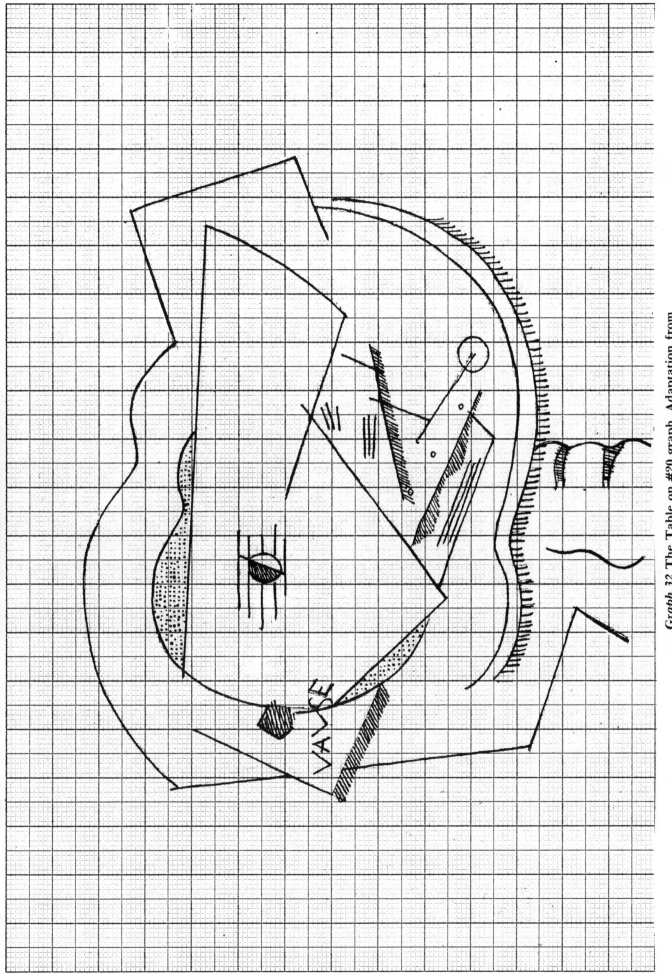

Graph 32 The Table on #20 graph. Adaptation from the etching by Henri Laurens (Photograph 17)

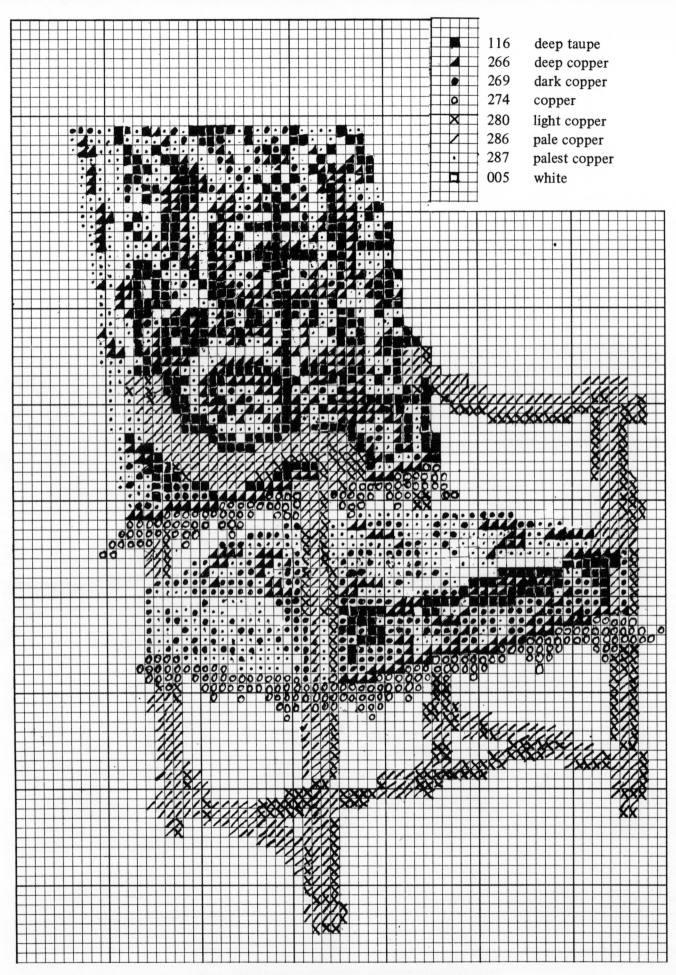

Graph 33 **The Chair on #10 graph. Adaptation of a Louis XIII chair. *Collection of Musée du Louvre* (Musée des Arts Decoratifs)**

The legend in the image reads:

■	116	deep taupe
◪	266	deep copper
◑	269	dark copper
○	274	copper
✕	280	light copper
╱	286	pale copper
•	287	palest copper
▫	005	white

a. 3¼ x 3¼ in. on #16 canvas

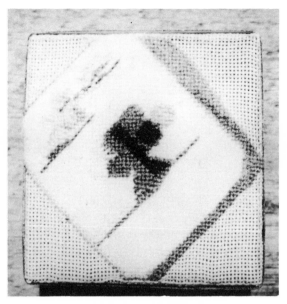

b. 3½ x 3½ in. on #16 canvas

c. 3½ x 3½ in. on #10/20 canvas

d. 3½ x 3½ in. on #12/24 canvas

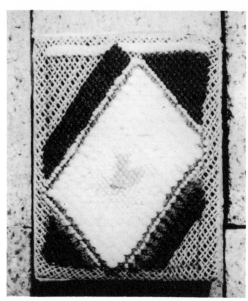

e. 4½ x 3½ in. on # 5/10 canvas

f. 4½ x 4½ in. on #16 canvas

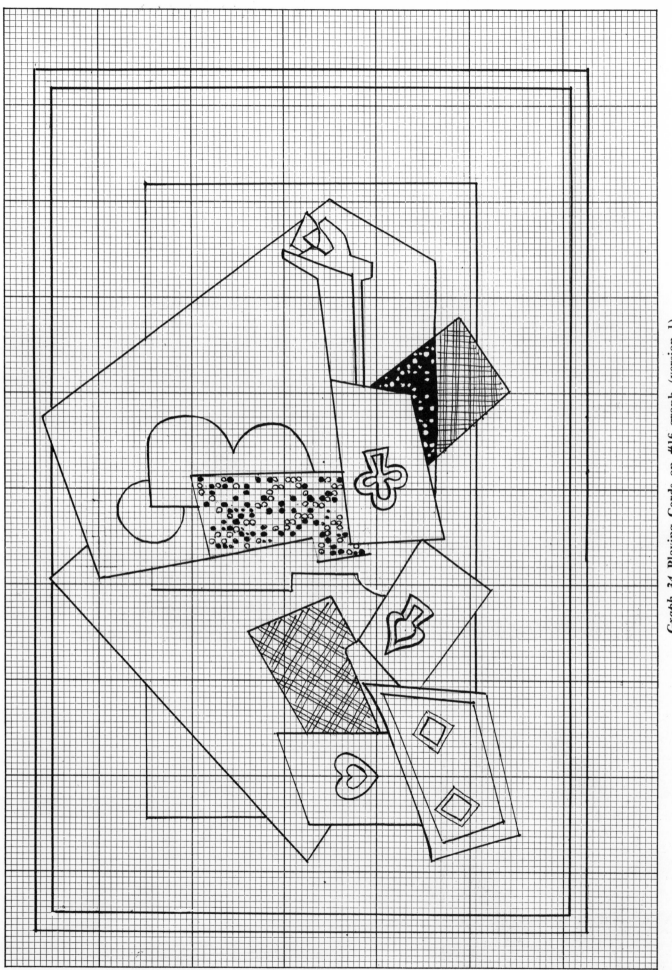

Graph 34 Playing Cards on #16 graph (version 1). Adaptation of the lithograph by Gino Severini. Collection of the author

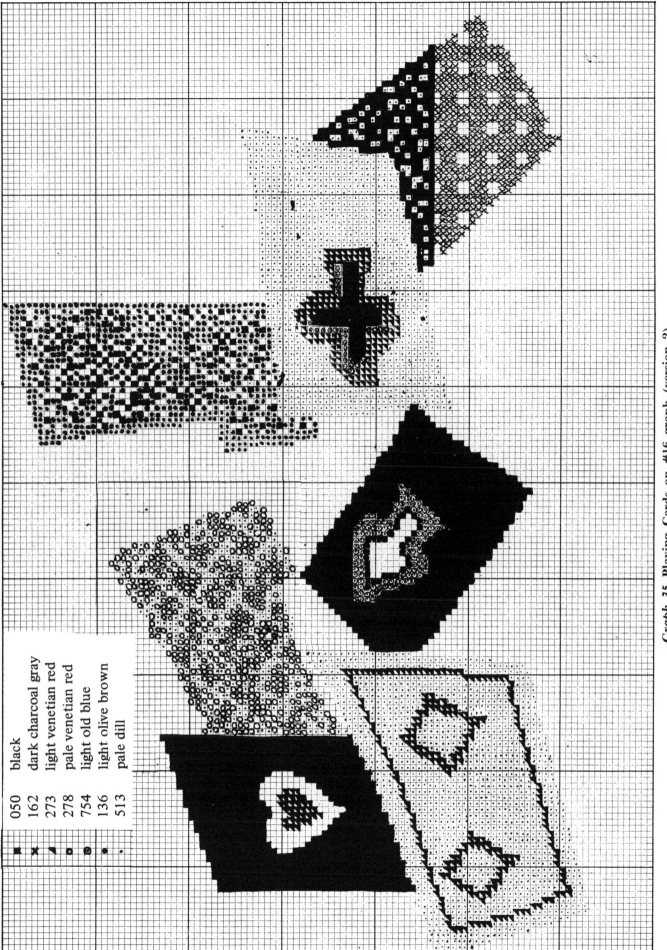

	050	black
	162	dark charcoal gray
	273	light venetian red
	278	pale venetian red
	754	light old blue
	136	light olive brown
	513	pale dill

Graph 35 **Playing Cards on #16 graph (version 2).** Adaptation of the lithograph by Gino Severini. *Collection of the author*

26
Sequence of a Zinnia

The sequence is from photo to line to enlarging by "squaring off" to design.

In the Zinnia (Fig. 19, Plate XXIII) just the photograph was traced in line, then enlarged to 13″ in diameter for a 14″ pillow. Then, to turn the flower into a design, "target" stripes were introduced in a rough sketch, experimenting with changes in line, color, and mass where the petals cross the border. The bands can be established by using a large compass or a string and pencil, or free hand, on a 17″ square of 16 point canvas painted with acrylic yellow.

The canvas with the edges taped was superimposed over the enlargement and the petals were freely outlined on the canvas. (If a photostat enlargement is used, first clarify the outline of the petals in India ink, because photostats lack contrast.)

After the basic design is made, and the decision that each circular band will be restricted to specific colors, and each petal is outlined, then, as you go along, work out the shading on each petal. This makes for a certain suspense. Everything doesn't have to be laid out beforehand.

Starting from the center of the canvas, the variations can be established in progress. Line? Color? Shading? As each band is established, a contrast is planned. Line changes to mass, pale blue to navy, to set off one band against another.

NOTE: In using acrylics, mix paint well with just enough water to make it flow on the canvas to cover well and yet not clog the holes.

Fig. 19   The zinnia

27
Sequence of a Rose

Unequaled through the centuries is the rose as an inspiration for flower textiles, wallpapers, and paintings, possibly because it is so well designed that in itself it is a drawing.

Here are some examples from photograph to graph that I hope will inspire you to try your own.

As with the Zinnia, first came the photograph, then the photostat, but in this case the latter was simplified preparatory to doing the collage version, breaking down still further the gray, black, and white shapes into more abstract patterns (Fig. 20).

Next a #20 graph paper was superimposed over the collage to make a petit point version (Graph 36).

Linear Rose is an outline rendition of Graph 36, repeated three times with the center in detail. The two surrounding details could act as shadows (Graph 37).

Shadow Rose is the rose of Graph 36 on #5 graph paper, which enlarges it four times, and this time it is shaded in the manner of an early textile (Graph 38 a and b).

The white chalk drawing of a rose on black paper was executed over a photograph (on a light table), simplifying the rose and emphasizing the form. Over this was placed a #10 graph paper and filled in accordingly (Graph 39, stages 1 and 2).

Next #16 graph paper was superimposed over the #10 graph and again a petit point version was made, blocking it in roughly and then removing it from the light table. Using symbols, light, medium, and dark, it was copied as closely as possible to the #10 graph, filling in the squares at the ratio of 16 to 10 (Graph 40).

Finally, see Frontispiece and Graph 1 (Rose is a rose . . .), which incorporate the rose (Graph 39, stage 2). You might try a petit point rose in the center. In using the #10 canvas, you would want to use the rose on #20 graph.

As you can see, there are many variations on the same theme. Try some interpretations of your own.

Fig. 20 The rose (photostat and collage)

Graph 36 Rose on #20 graph

Graph 37 Rose, Linear, on #20 graph

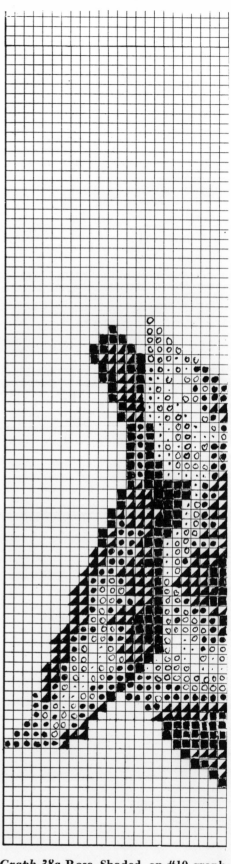

Graph 38a Rose, Shaded, on #10 graph

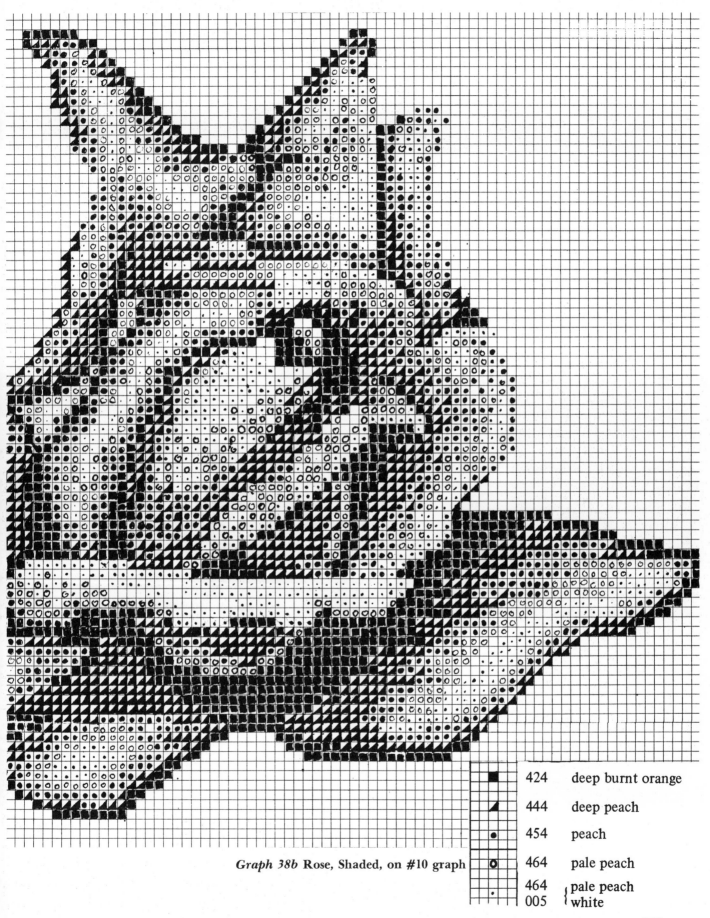

	424	deep burnt orange
	444	deep peach
	454	peach
	464	pale peach
	464	{ pale peach
	005	{ white

Graph 38b Rose, Shaded, on #10 graph

125

Graph 39 Rose, Stages 1 and 2

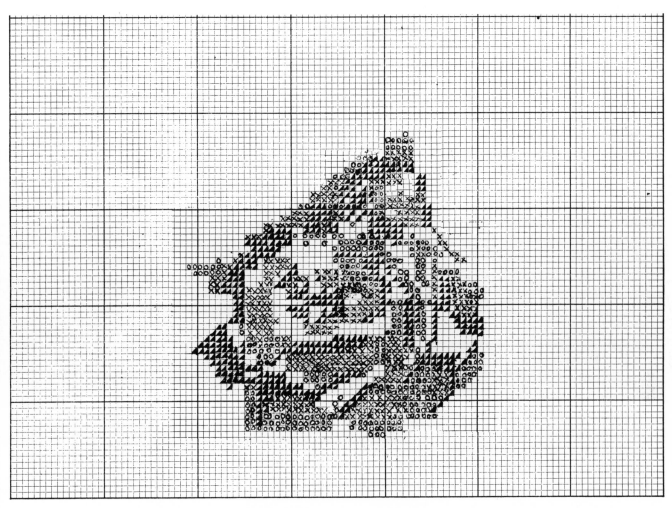

Graph 40 The Rose on #16 graph

28
From Petit Point to Gros Point or Vice Versa

Petit point as a combination with gros point can only be done on penelope canvas. Spread the vertical thread apart in the area where you are going to do the petit point. Accuracy doesn't matter here; you can always keep spreading or pushing together again if you have gone too far.

Spreading the penelope will mean that you are working over single threads, making it the same as mono, and if you do the basket weave in petit point, look back at chapter 10, Hazards of Basket Weave on Mono Canvas.

Try a simple design first, like the leaf in Figure 21. Since this is your first attempt, use the Continental. After you have completed the leaf, try surrounding it with gros point. Usually I advise surrounding the design with more petit point in a background color in an extension of the same shape, or another shape, like a square or a circle, as shown throughout the book. But for the sake of space in this enlarged drawing I am showing the object surrounded by gros point in the conventional way.

Some needlepointers advocate doing the gros point background up to the object and then filling in the leftover holes that are bound to exist. Others fill in the odd petit point holes with the background color first and then do the gros point. Try both to see which you prefer.

In the penelope, two verticals and two horizontals create an intersection of four threads. This intersection must be free for a gros point stitch to encompass. If one of these four intersections has a petit point stitch, then the other three must be in petit point in the *background* color.

Some of the gros point, petit point illustrations are done on 6 point (quickie) so the petit point is 12 stitches to the inch, which of course is *not* petit point. But since the chief concern is how we go from a 12 point to a 6 point, or 10 point to 5 point (and the same rule would apply to a petit point 24 point to 12), it seems less confusing to call a stitch *petit* any time *it is contrasted* to a large stitch on the same canvas.

Fig. 21   From petit point to gros point

29
Reading Graphs

In reading graphs it's important to realize a few generalities.

Some of the original designs brought together here had more colors than seemed necessary, so simplifications have been made. Others, like Graph 41a, b, seemed to lose individual appeal by simplification, so in some cases you will be using a luxurious number of yarns.

Designs like the one just mentioned have been carefully matched to Paternayan yarns so that an exact replica can be made. Others are more generally stated and it is left to the reader to determine the exact shade.

In another case, where there is a large flat area, the symbols, once established, have not been followed through, for it is obvious that it is a repeat of the one color in each area (Graph 42a, b). In some cases, like the house in Graph 59 and Plate XXXI, the needlepointer can either carry out the design consistently or possibly vary it. After completing the yellow symbols you might move into a deeper or paler yellow.

And again, variations rather than a flat brown area in the Coptic rabbit (Plate VI) give the illusion of different dyes so typical of early textiles.

The graph drawings in this book are divided into two categories.

a. These graphs adhere to the squares of the graph paper so the finished canvas will not vary much in contours, spirals, circles, etcetera. As you work on a bare canvas using the graph as a guide, your main concern will be following each grid, counting correctly as you do it.

b. The freehand drawings ignore the graph squares. You will trace these designs directly on the canvas (as they are, or enlarged).

Then, as you start to work the canvas, some holes are obviously to be filled in—others are questionable. Where the line divides the square in two, you will have to make an on-the-spot decision about whether to ignore it or to fill it in.

Indian Floral (Graph 44) and Floral on Silk (Plate XXIV, Graph 43a, b) both lend themselves to being enlarged by photostat, traced on canvas, and executed with on-the-spot decisions, as explained above.

Faces are more crucial than florals when it comes to detail. For instance, there were many trials and errors on graph paper before the exact number of squares was established for capturing a likeness of Tinkle (Graph 3a). It is much better to make the changes on graph paper than on the actual canvas.

Floral on Silk is one of the more complex of the line drawings. Have it photostated, or square it off up to the size you desire, then trace it onto your canvas. Fill in the strongest lines first, then add as much or as little detail as you please.

In a gradation of symbols that calls for something like five shades of the same color, remember that in using two strands for example, three colors—A, B, and C—will make five shades by mixing the strands:

AA, AB, BB, BC, CC

Three strands will produce even more variety:

AAA, AAB, ABB, BBB, BBC, BCC, CCC

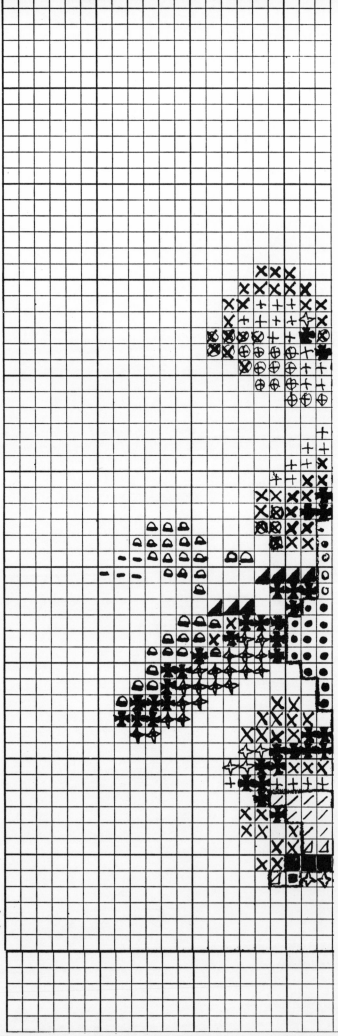

	113	charcoal brown
	262	deep old rose
	283	old rose
	870	palest pink
	217	deep cinnamon
	215	dark venetian red
	273	light venetian red

	427	deep gold
	Y42	carat gold
	172	toast
	174	light toast
	194	pale toast
	311	deep slate blue
	330	delft blue

	641	pale violet
	612	dark wood violet
	127	mauve
	137	light mauve
	381	light slate blue
	395	palest delft
	311	(background) deep slate blue

Graphs 41a and 41b **Doorstop on #6 graph. Adaptation of a doorstop.** *Collection of the Wenham Historical Society*

132

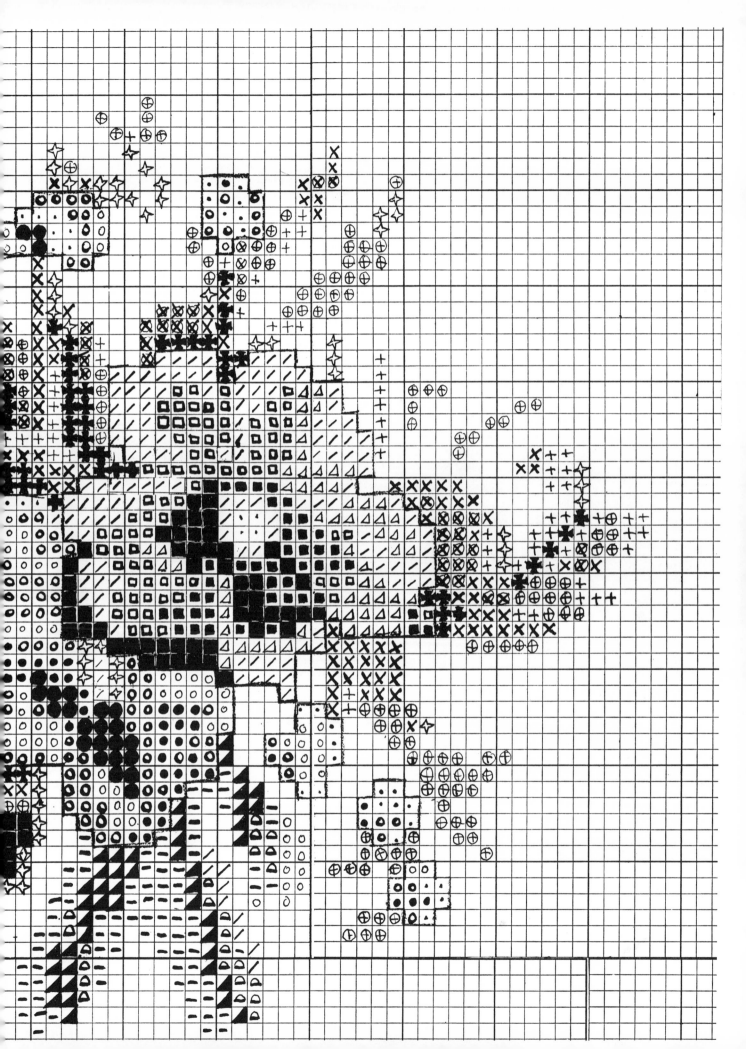

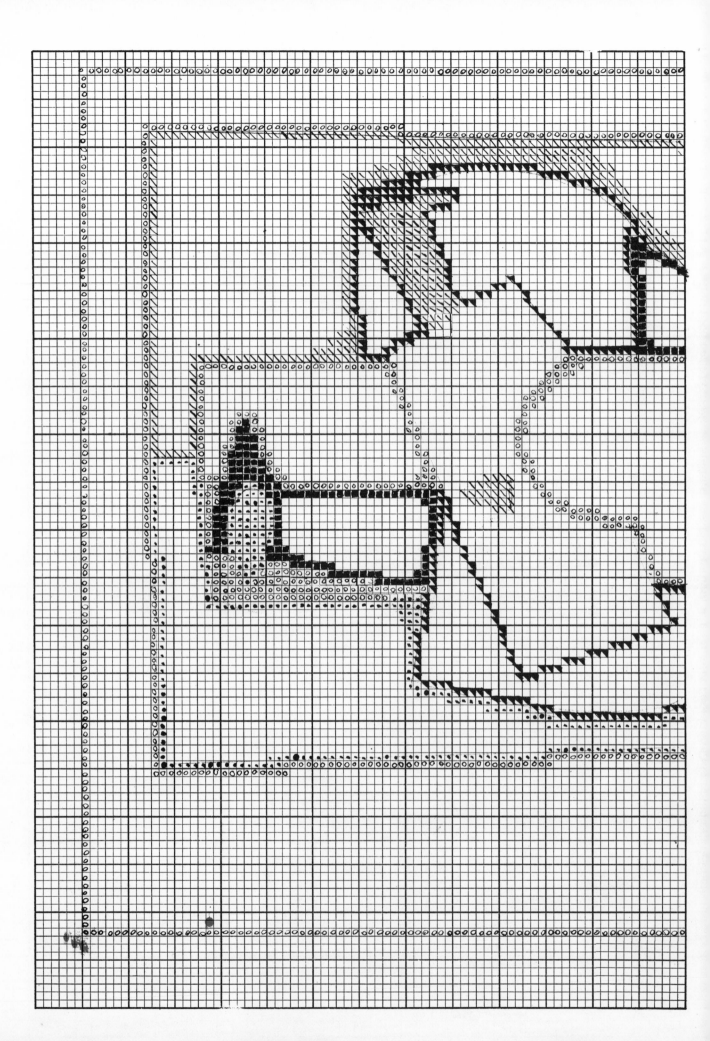

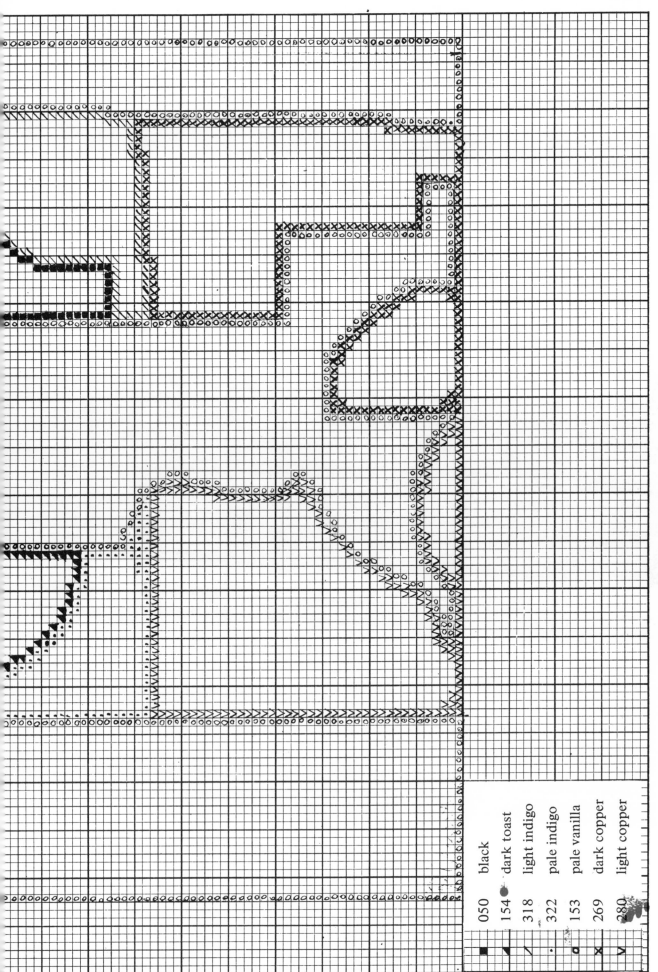

Graphs 42a and 42b **The White Table on #12 graph.**
Adaptation from The White Table, 1923, Pablo
Picasso. *Collection of Mrs. John Winterseen*

■	050	black
◣	154	dark toast
⁄	318	light indigo
·	322	pale indigo
◲	153	pale vanilla
✕	269	dark copper
⋁	280	light copper

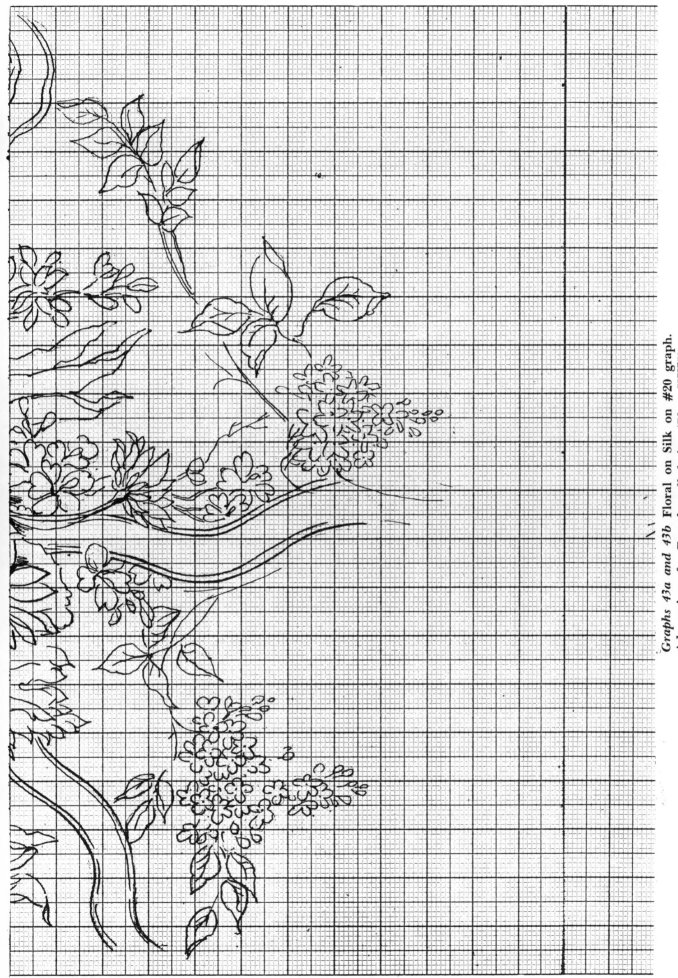

Graphs 43a and 43b Floral on Silk on #20 graph. Adaptation of a French wall design (Plate XXIV)

Graph 44 Indian Floral on *#20* graph. Adaptation from an Indian embroidery. *Collection of the Museum of Fine Arts, Boston, Massachusetts*

30
Simplicity of Design

Just remember this: simplicity can be dramatic.

An easy piano piece well played, or a simple turn on the ice expertly executed is often more effective and exciting than difficult passages and jump turns that lack top performance.

Don't be afraid of large areas of white. A design that can breathe and not have every inch accounted for looks alive and as if it had been great fun to do.

One of the pitfalls of earnest designers and the greatest way to kill spontaneity is to make over-complicated patterns.

For an exercise in simplicity try Figure 22. This oval design is good practice and makes a handsome trivet.

Try this Peaches design (Graph 45) too, with its great expanse of off-white areas. See if you don't capture the simplicity and floating quality created by such an expanse of one shade.

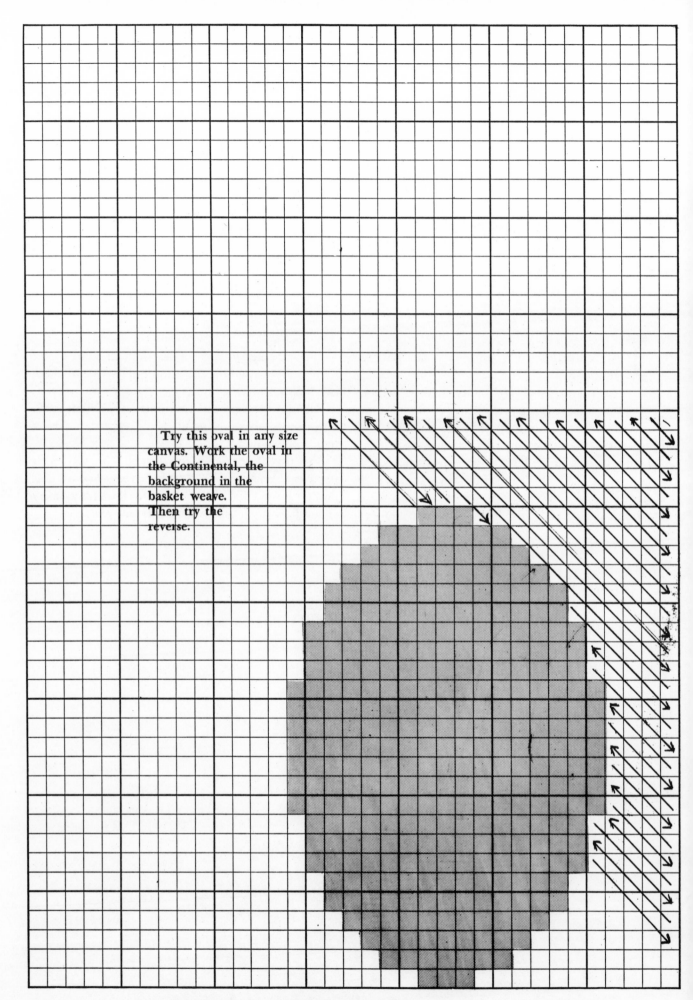

Try this oval in any size
canvas. Work the oval in
the Continental, the
background in the
basket weave.
Then try the
reverse.

Fig. 22   Oval design

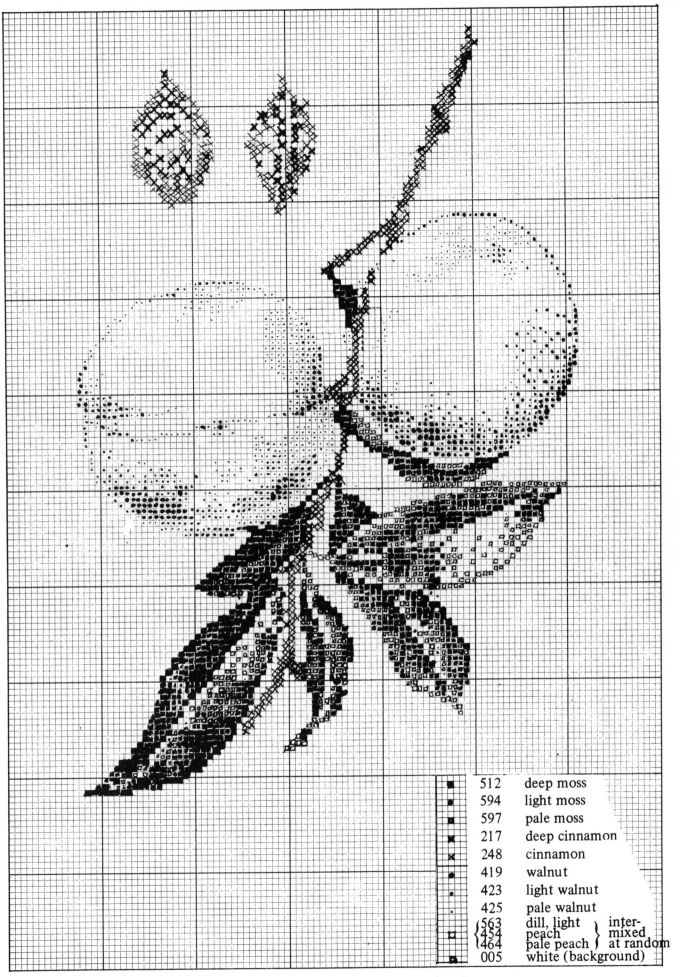

	512	deep moss
	594	light moss
	597	pale moss
	217	deep cinnamon
	248	cinnamon
	419	walnut
	423	light walnut
	425	pale walnut
	563	dill, light } inter-
	454	peach } mixed
	464	pale peach } at random
	005	white (background)

Graph 45 **Peaches on #16 graph. Adaptation from the horticultural book** *Peaches of New York*

31
General Rules for Working the Graphs

As you travel from RIGHT to LEFT and DOWN on the canvas, always start with the object nearest the upper right-hand corner. From there go to the next object, working your way down to the lower left-hand side. Work each object from the center out. In a subject like a rose with three or more shades, thread as many needles as there are colors involved. After the center of the flower is finished, start on an adjacent color, spreading away from the center.

Usually it is best not to jump around with the same color, because an unworked area wedged in between two worked sections may not have room for the required number of stitches. In other words, there is less chance of a mistake if you spread away from the worked stitches. Sometimes a stem or a line in the design will help you get from one object to another. Try to let any error fall in the background, where one stitch more or less doesn't matter.

With a small object (Fig. 33) fill in solidly rather than outline, and with a large object, outline it first (Graph 47).

In an outline, when you come back to the place where you started, it can be very upsetting to find that your stitches don't meet as they should. This is why constant checking back should be done. Sometimes you can reorganize the last 12 stitches or so to make them connect with the start of the design.

32

A Few Rules on Composition

Rules for composition do exist, but mostly it is a case of trial and error and continually working at it.

The subject matter and how you decide to handle it is 75% of the challenge, with decisions to make about color, value, line against mass, and so on.

The remaining 25% is usually a case of good luck or bad. When a design is going well, extra dividends accrue with unexpected relationships happening, often better than expected. Bad luck is when a design has every reason to be good and just seems to miss.

Let us take a circle in a rectangle and see the different effects that come about by the placement (Fig. 23):

a. A circle in the center is usually to be avoided unless it seems affected to have it otherwise. In Graph 1 it would attract unnecessary attention to have the rose off center, making the words too prominent in one place.

b. In placing the circle above the center, there is an illusion of floating.

c. When the circle is lower than the center, a feeling of weight occurs.

d. A divided circle creates still another effect, appearing to control space outside the rectangle.

Now, if the circle is made into a flower form, the stems and leaves can be worked into a design to create an effect of space, or allover pattern, or even distance, all depending on how these details are handled.

1. A mass of leaves in one corner will create space in another.

2. Hints of a distant landscape or the sea will also promote a sense of space.

3. Stems and leaves rhythmically filling in the whole area like a Persian or Chinese dish will create an allover pattern that has its own drama.

Try all three of these ideas to see which you like the best.

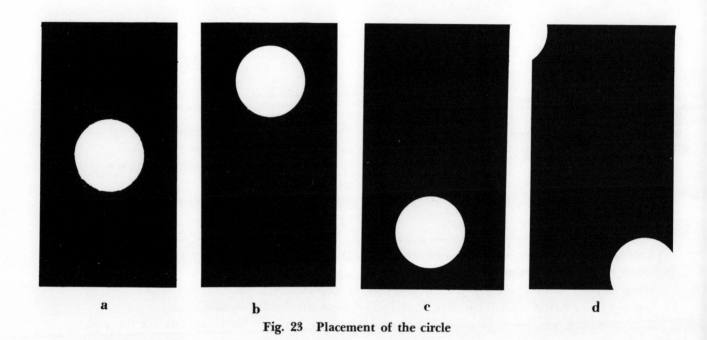

a   b   c   d

Fig. 23   Placement of the circle

Plate XXIV Floral on Silk. Philippe de LA SALLE
Tissu de soie, *Eighteenth-Century Collection Musée
Historique des Tissus, Lyon, France* (Graphs 43a and
43b) *Photograph by Photographie Giraudon*

Plate XXV Mr. Tod. 11½ x 11½ in. on #14 canvas. Designed and worked by Betsy Wiederhold (Graph 49)

Plate XXVI Piet Mondrian. Composition in Black and Gray (detail) 7½ x 7½ in. on #12 canvas. Worked by Eleanor Hempstead (Graph 48, Photograph 21)

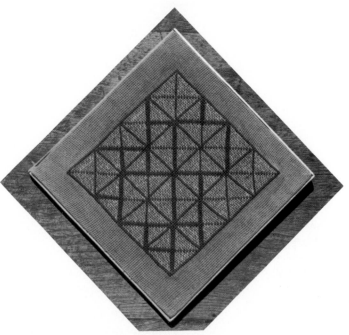

Plate XXVII Piet Mondrian. Composition in Black and Gray (detail) 7½ x 7½ in. on #12 canvas. Worked by Betsy Wiederhold (Graph 48, Photograph 21)

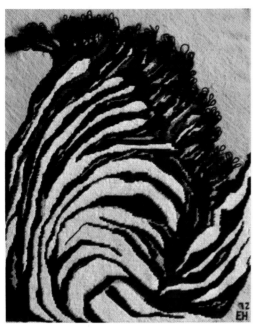

Plate XXVIII Zebra. 17½ x 14½ in. on #14 canvas. Designed and worked by Eleanor Hempstead. *Photograph by Barbara Sutro*

Plate XXX Chinese Motifs. 24 x 9 in. on #14 canvas. Designed and worked by James Ziegler (Graphs 53, 54) *Photograph by Barbara Sutro*

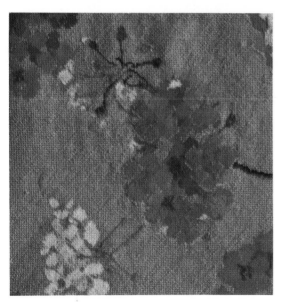

Plate XXIX Geraniums. 19 x 14 in. on #14 canvas. Designed and worked by James Ziegler. *Photograph by Barbara Sutro*

Plate **XXXI** King Caesar House. Duxbury, Massachusetts (Graph 59)

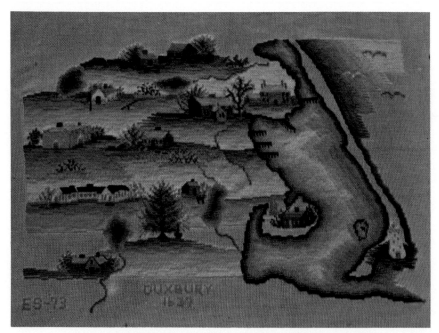

Plate **XXXII** Map Landscape. 16 x 21 in. on #14 canvas. Designed and worked by Elisabeth W. Sears

33
What Are You Making?

The question should be—What are you designing?

For instance, if you say to an artist, "What are you painting?" he immediately answers, "A still life," "an abstraction," "a nude," or whatever; he doesn't say, "I'm painting a *picture.*"

But with needlepoint, particularly if it's a small portable canvas that can be whipped out at random in buses, subways, skating rinks, parks, beaches, theaters, and so on, and therefore seen by the passer-by, the question always is *WHAT* are you making?

So I, on purpose, misinterpret by saying "a Coptic rabbit," or "a variation on the ace of clubs," and the impatient bystander insists, "But *what is* it?" So, unfortunately, you give in and find yourself saying, "It's a pincushion!"

34
Enlarging–Photostat, Lucida

The most accurate and fastest way to *enlarge* or *reduce* a design to your desired dimensions is by means of the photostat or lucida.

The latter is an amazing precision instrument that enables the viewer to see his design reflected on the drawing board in the exact size he wishes (see chapter 55).

The photostat, unlike the Xerox machine, is usually found only in cities, though it is worth inquiring around. The photostats are not inexpensive, like Xeroxes, but are far less than photographic enlargements.

First a negative print is made from your design and then a positive. Sometimes a negative print (Fig. 40 in chapter 50, The Tailored Look) is adequate and just as easy to work from. Simply remember that white reproduces as black.

Be very careful to decide *exactly* how much of the design you want enlarged and the exact number of inches it should take up.

For direct transfer to the canvas, place the negative or positive photostat on the light table (or some substitute) and make a tracing with strong lines and clear details. Then remove the photostat and place the canvas over the new rendering. Trace the design onto your canvas with pencil or the NEPO pen (see chapter 41).

As mentioned earlier, sometimes the photostat hasn't enough contrast or clear lines to trace from it directly onto the canvas, so strengthen the lines with India ink.

For a graph rendition, place graph paper over the photostat or the new tracing and, using symbols like those throughout the book, fill in the various squares. You will soon discover that the larger the graph squares, the easier to make the symbols.

Enlarging by squaring off, the oldest technique used by the old masters, is a last resort, what with more modern means. It can be most time consuming, particularly if a face or figure is involved—$1/8$ of an inch can turn a fat cat into a thin cat!

For florals and other less definite shapes the accuracy isn't so critical.

Figure 19 (chapter 26, Sequence of the Zinnia) shows the theory of squaring off.

35
Gauging the Size of the Design

Fourteen point canvas actually measures 13 holes to the inch. It is sold as 14 or 13 point, depending on the manufacturer.

No. 13 graph is sold in packages in the stationery and five and ten cent stores.

Sometimes you may want to make a graph design but have no graph paper that corresponds in size to the canvas you want to use. Then adjustments must be made.

Study Figure 24. Here is a pear 65 *stitches* long from stem to stern. It swells and shrinks according to the size graph it is on. The more holes to the inch, the smaller it is; the fewer holes to the inch, the larger. The *key* is that the *number* of *stitches* remains the *same* on each graph.

In planning a needlepoint, count the number of holes your design is to take up, which is easy because you know the *size* of your canvas is the *number* of holes to the inch.

Keep studying the pears and study the differences in length on the various graphs.

Remember that a design on 5 graph will be half the size on 10 point canvas.

Suppose you want a design *10″* long on 14 point canvas and all you have is *8″* graph. *Eight x 10* is 80 and so that will be the number of squares you will use on your graph lengthwise.

When you work it on the 14 point canvas, the design will contract to its planned size. Eighty squares filled in on 5″ graph would be (5 into 80) 16″ long, so the graphs would have to be taped together, but this is often good since it affords larger squares in which to make notations.

If you enlarge a petit point done on 20 graph to 5″ graph, it will of course enlarge 4 times and again necessitate taping sheets together.

If you have only 8″ graph that has a heavy line to mark off each inch, again count off 80 squares; ignore the heavy lines. Instead, with a colored pen draw a heavy line every 10 squares. Naturally it is preferable to have graph without the heavy lines—unless it corresponds to what you are using, as, in this case, 10 squares to the inch.

But it seems to be increasingly difficult to get just what you want in the way of graph paper unless you are in the city, so I am trying to show that any graph will do as long as you remember the *key*. That is, the number of *stitches* must correspond to the number of *squares*.

NOTE: The butterfly from the Metropolitan Museum (Graph 46, Plate V) was originally a cross-stitch 1″ high, consisting of 60 stitches. By transferring it to 10 point canvas it becomes 6″ high because 6 x 10 = 60!

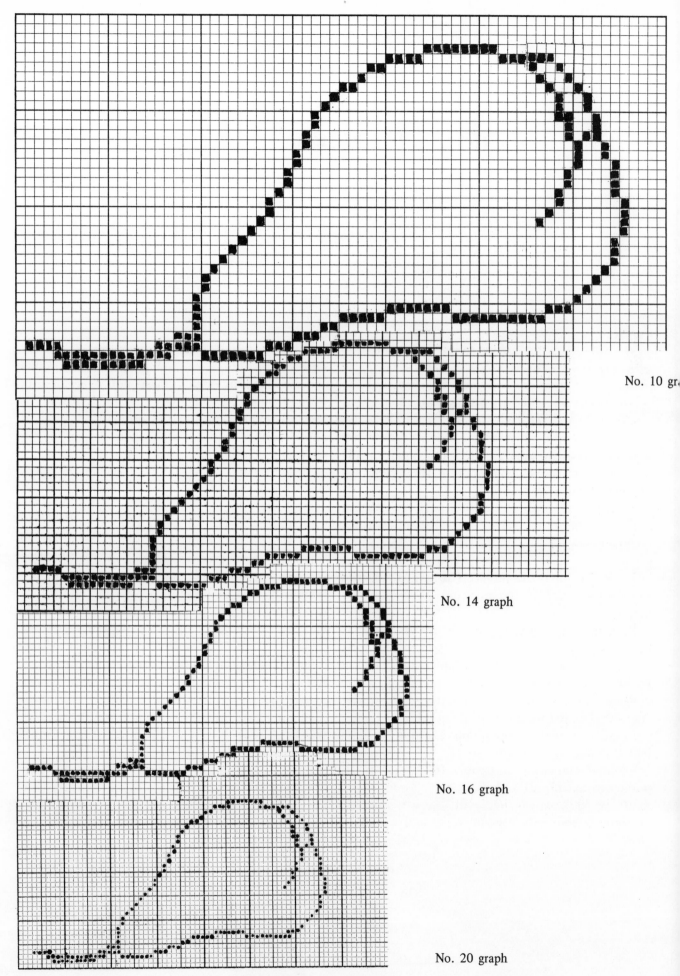

No. 10 gr

No. 14 graph

No. 16 graph

No. 20 graph

Fig. 24 The pear

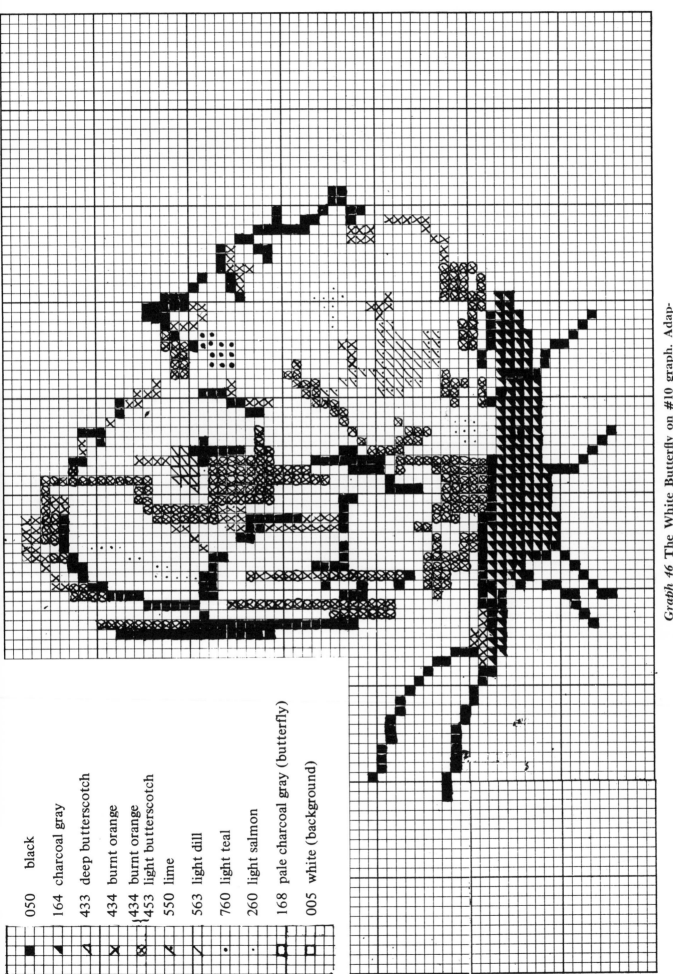

Graph 46 **The White Butterfly on #10 graph. Adaptation of a Nineteenth-Century Austrian sampler, design 1 in. high.** *Collection of the Metropolitan Museum of Art* **(Plate V)**

050   black

164   charcoal gray

433   deep butterscotch

434   burnt orange

{434   burnt orange
453   light butterscotch

550   lime

563   light dill

760   light teal

260   light salmon

168   pale charcoal gray (butterfly)

005   white (background)

36
Don't Be Afraid of Being a Pro

ften there is a tendency to hide behind the protective skirts of remaining a tyro or novice and to shy away from the expense of top materials. Professional means professional equipment output, whether in sports, crafts, or whatever.

An important part of needlepoint designing is a "light table" or tracing box.

The primitive forerunner is the windowpane method, where the sketch is taped to the glass and, because of the strong light outside, it is possible to make a fresh outline on the superimposed tracing paper.

The light table is a box about 16″ x 20″ with a fluorescent light inside covered with a "ground" glass that gives a translucent effect.

It is invaluable for tracing designs from books, magazines, catalogues, and, of course, is most helpful not only in tracing your finished outline from your rough sketch but also in transferring the outline to the canvas.

When tracing from magazines and other pictures and photographs, have a xerox or, if you are enlarging, a photostat made, because the reverse side of the printed page shows through.

If you are a needlepointer who works on the pure canvas from graph paper, the light table is important in transferring your sketch onto graph paper.

I saw an ingenious home-constructed light table—a piece of glass simply taped onto a frame, hinged to a drawing board (Fig. 25).

The frame in this case was originally for a silk screen, but a carpenter could make a strong frame for you to hold the glass.

Painting directly onto a canvas without a clear idea can lead to changes that can play havoc and make an unpleasant surface to work on.

With the white canvas superimposed over the clearly defined sketch, sure strokes in flat paint, acrylic, or oil can be established immediately without the danger of overworked areas.

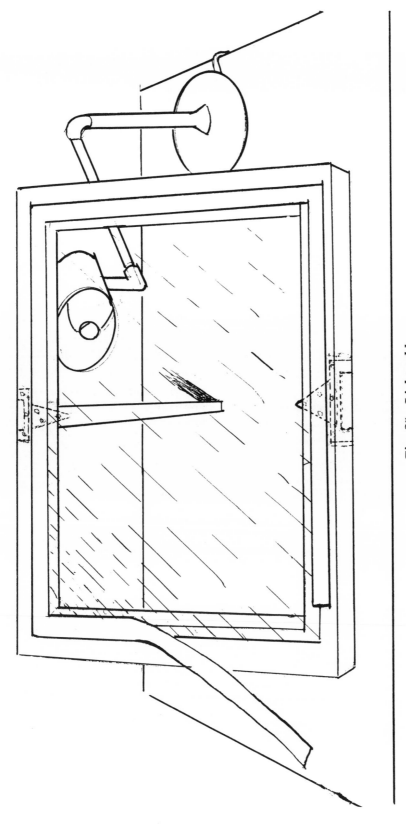

Fig. 25 Light table

37
A Picture, before Being a Warhorse . . .

Maurice Denis, the artist, said, "A picture, before being a warhorse, a female nude or some anecdote, is essentially a flat surface covered with colors assembled in a particular order."

This analysis offers good advice, not only for a painter, but for anyone concerned with good design. A basic rule for needlepoint is—"Would you like to sit on it?" This should curb too-realistic flowers, animals, and so on.

In one of the two Picasso chair designs (Photograph 19), the chalk-white silhouette of a hand is placed between a dark background and a free foliage design, like a découpage.

The other chair is a statement in space and simplicity, adroitly controlled by a shadow.

In both cases it is the *combination* of simple motifs, the hand and the foliage, the molding and the shadow, that turns good design into a masterpiece of wit, enchantment, and originality.

Genius is often as simple as this.

Photograph 19 Two Needlepoint Chairs. Designs for needlepoint by Pablo Picasso, executed by Alice B. Toklas as upholstery for two eighteenth-century chairs (late 1920s). *Collection, American Literature, Beinecke Rare Book and Manuscript Library, Yale University, New Haven, Connecticut*

Photograph 20 Stag. Coptic, Sixth Century A.D. *The Brooklyn Museum, Gift of Colonel Robert S. Woodward* (Graph 47)

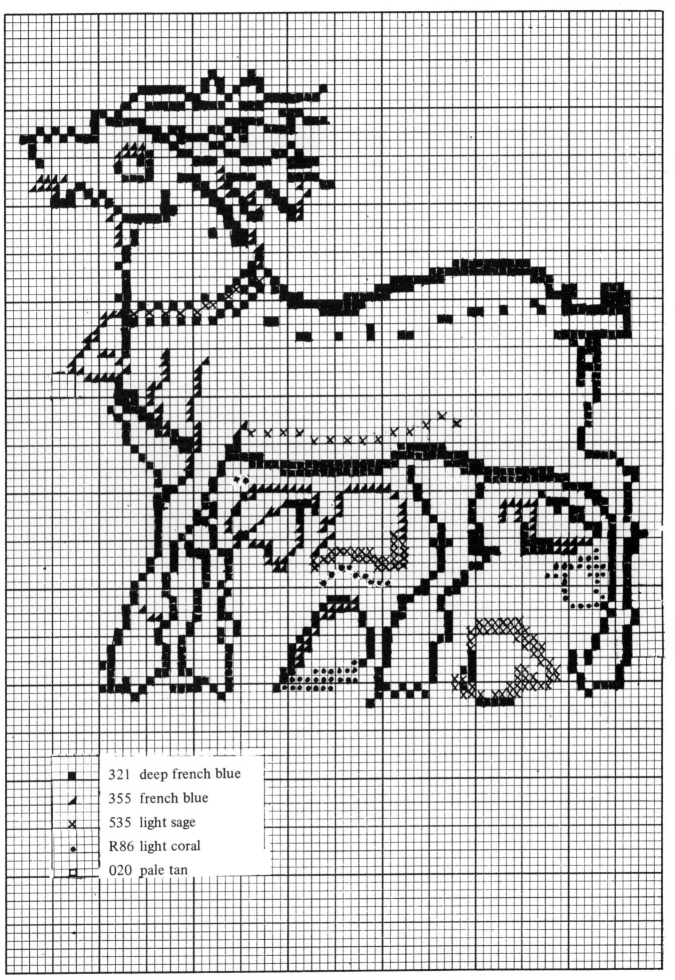

321 deep french blue

355 french blue

535 light sage

R86 light coral

020 pale tan

Graph 47 Stag on #12 graph. Adaptation of a Coptic
textile (Photograph 20)

38
Transferring Graph to Canvas

Xerox copies made from these designs are going to prove useful for transferring graph designs to canvas. Graph 47 is going to be our example of how to go about it. Look at Photograph 20 from which the graph design of the stag was made.

Place a piece of tracing paper over the numbered work sheet (Fig. 26) and trace the lines with a ruler and the numbers freely, then tape the tracing paper to the xerox so it remains firm.

You will find that the superimposed tracing is only needed through square 56 (Fig. 27), since the stag design is almost square.

Find the center of your tracing by ruling from corner to corner, A to B and C to D, making short diagonal lines in the middle of the work sheet (Fig. 28). The center will be established where the diagonals cross.

Now cut a piece of 12 point canvas 14″ square preparatory to making a 10″ by 10″ pillow. Don't forget to tape the edges.

Draw parallel lines 2″ from the borders to make a 10″ by 10″ square.

Draw the first horizontal through the center of the canvas (Fig. 28) so it is 7″ long (3½″ to the right and 3½″ to the left). Keep on drawing parallel lines 1″ apart until you have 9 going across and 8 vertically. This will make up the 7″ by 8″ rectangle to correspond to the work sheet. Notice that the central verticals are ½″ to the right and to the left of the center.

Take two pieces of heavy paper like an index card and cut out a 1″ square hole and a 2″ square hole. The latter is used when your graph is double the size (Fig. 29a and c).

Now number your squares on the canvas to correspond to the tracing work sheet in pencil or NEPO. Warning: Sometimes, under very light or white areas of yarn, the NEPO shows through (this is not to be confused with the pen's bleeding and discoloring the yarn when wet), so sometimes a pencil is better.

Finally you are ready to begin. As we normally progress from right to left, let us start with the tail, which would be square 21* (Fig. 30). Lay the card with the 1″ hole over the square on the graph. The first stitch would be 2 holes up from the lower left hand corner of the square and 7 squares to the right (Fig. 29a). Now follow Fig. 30 for the sequence of stitches, remembering to go LEFT, DOWN, and DIAGONALLY in any direction, and to turn the canvas completely around when it is necessary to go RIGHT or UP. Lay your card with the 1″ square hole on the lettered diagram, for it is just the size of your original graph and canvas.

In Figure 31 follow the main part of the body *first;* leave antlers, eye, and details (marked in lower case) until later. When you come to the legs, work along the body to the foreleg on your right. Go down and up to meet where you started. Work other legs going left.

Here is a helpful hint. If it is only a question of going a few stitches UP or to the RIGHT, use the AMBI-D stitch described in the chapter on left-handed needlepoint. Since right-handed direc-

1	2	3	4	5	6	7
8	9	10	11	12	13	14
15	16	17	18	19	20	21
22	23	24	25	26	27	28
29	30	31	32	33	34	35
36	37	38	39	40	41	42
43	44	45	46	47	48	49
50	51	52	53	54	55	56
57	58	59	60	61	62	63
64	65	66	67	68	69	70

Fig. 26 NUMBERED WORK SHEET

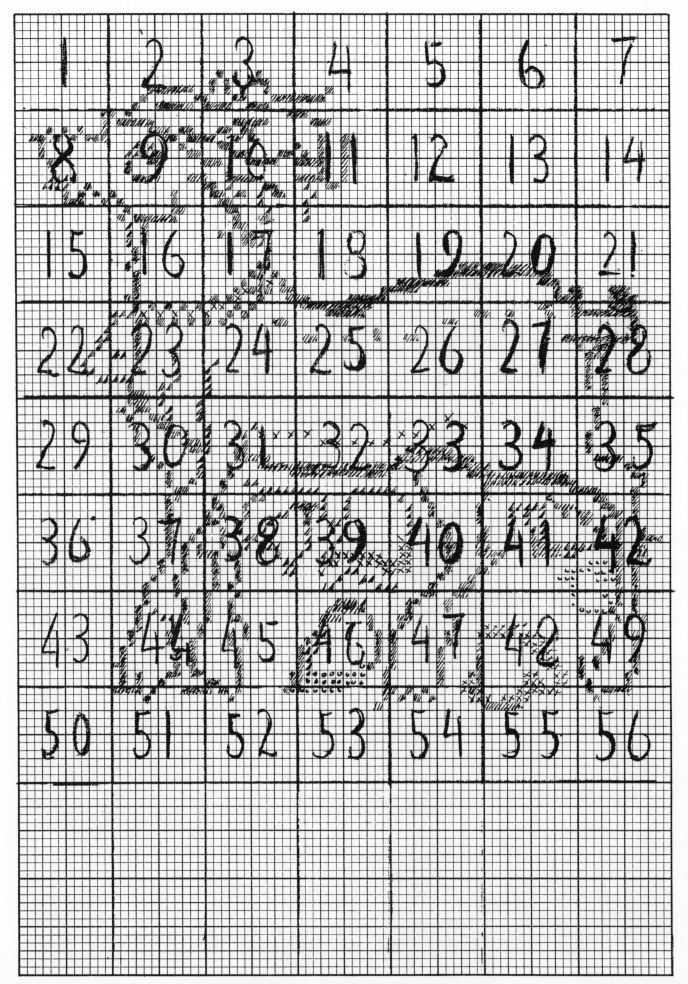

Fig. 27 Tracing of stag superimposed on #12 graph

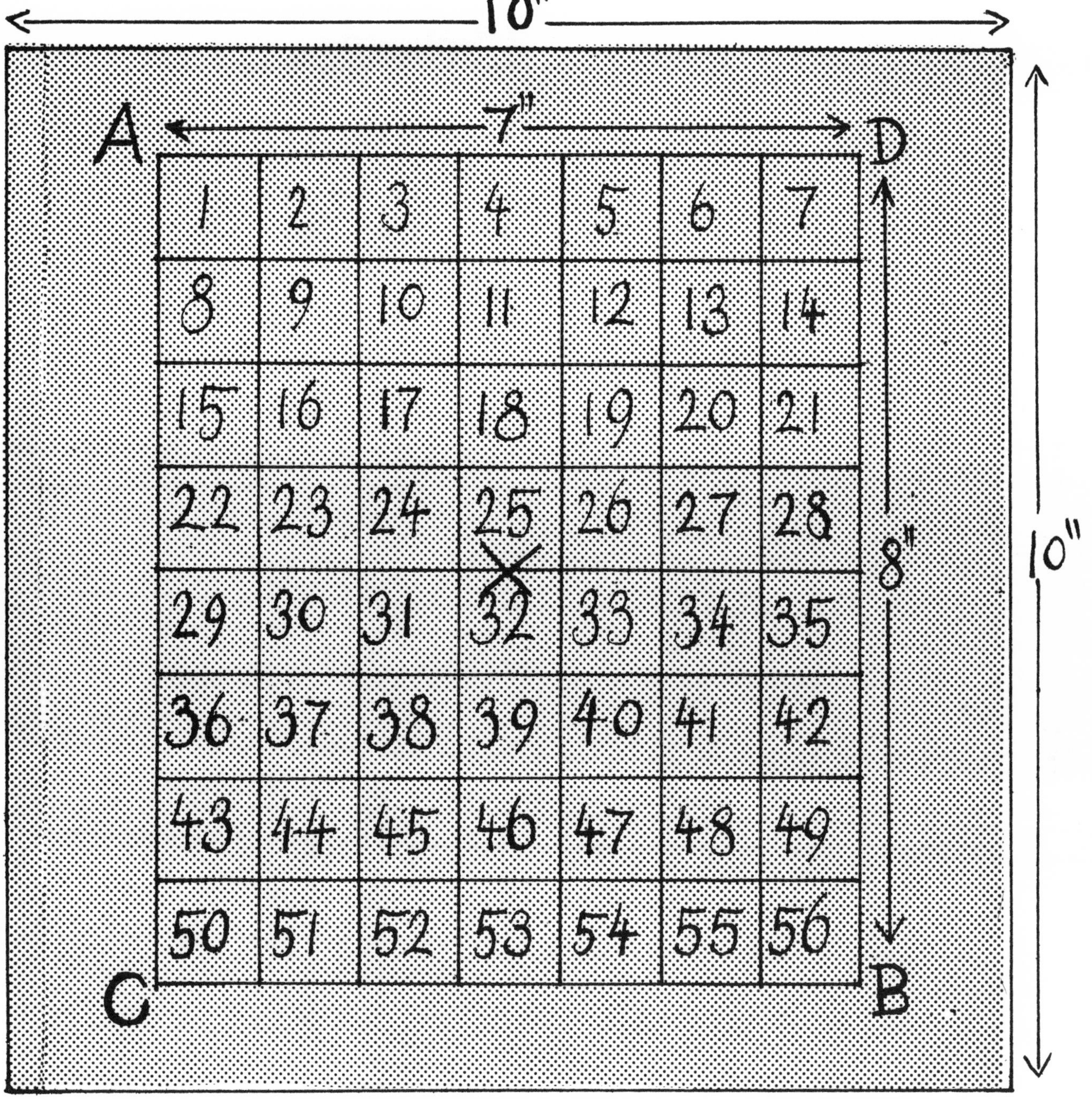

Fig. 28 Canvas pattern

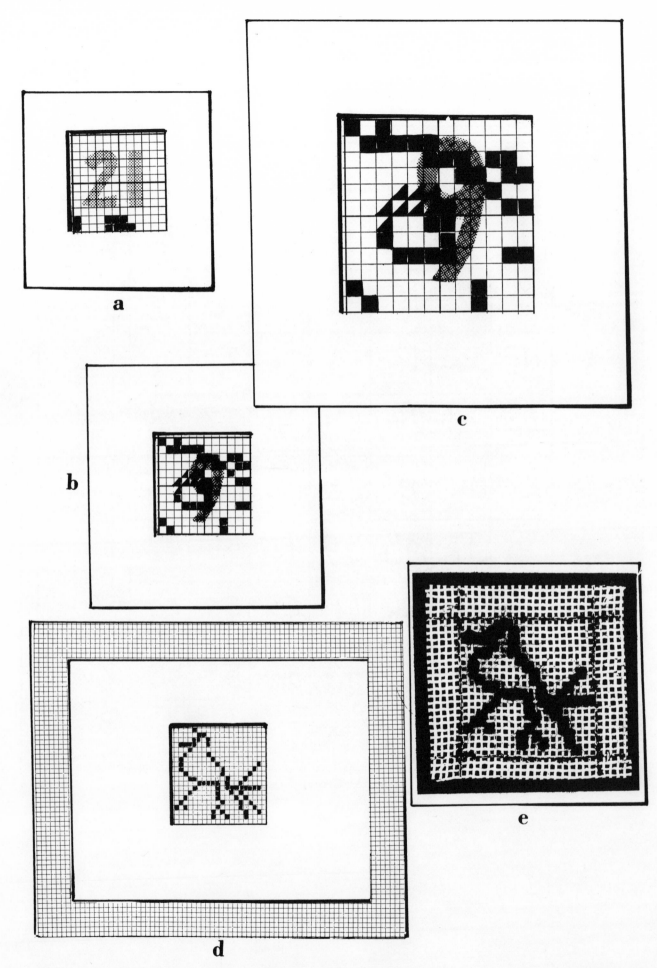

Fig. 29 Series of figures

tions are awkward for left-handers, this stitch in turn will be awkward for right-handers and will have to be done one stitch at a time. Do what is more comfortable for you, *turning the canvas around* or using the AMBI-D stitch.

To double the size of the graph "Stag" from #12 canvas (Fig. 29b), work the same design on #6 canvas (Fig. 29c). To make it half the size (which is approximately the size of the original textile), work it in petit point on #12 canvas, splitting the threads to make them 24 holes or stitches to the inch.

You can transfer this graph to ANY size canvas. Remember the pear! All you have to think about is having the same number of *holes* or *stitches* in the canvas as *squares* in the graph paper.

For instance, study the small motif of a bird (Fig. 29d). Transfer 20″ graph to 14 point canvas by measuring off 20 holes in the 14 point canvas (Fig. 29e). This will determine the space between the parallel lines on the canvas, which is slightly over 1½ inches.

To transfer from 20 graph to 16 point canvas would make 20 holes or stitches *exactly* 1¼ inches, so the parallel lines would be 1¼ inches apart.

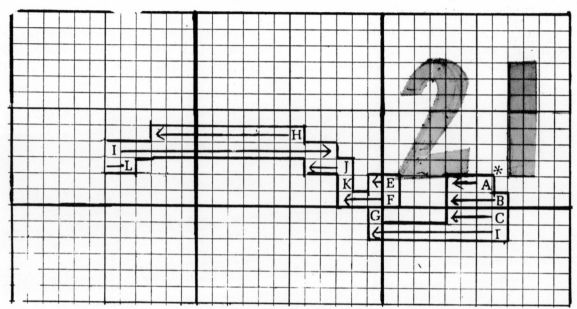

Fig. 30 Numbered stag

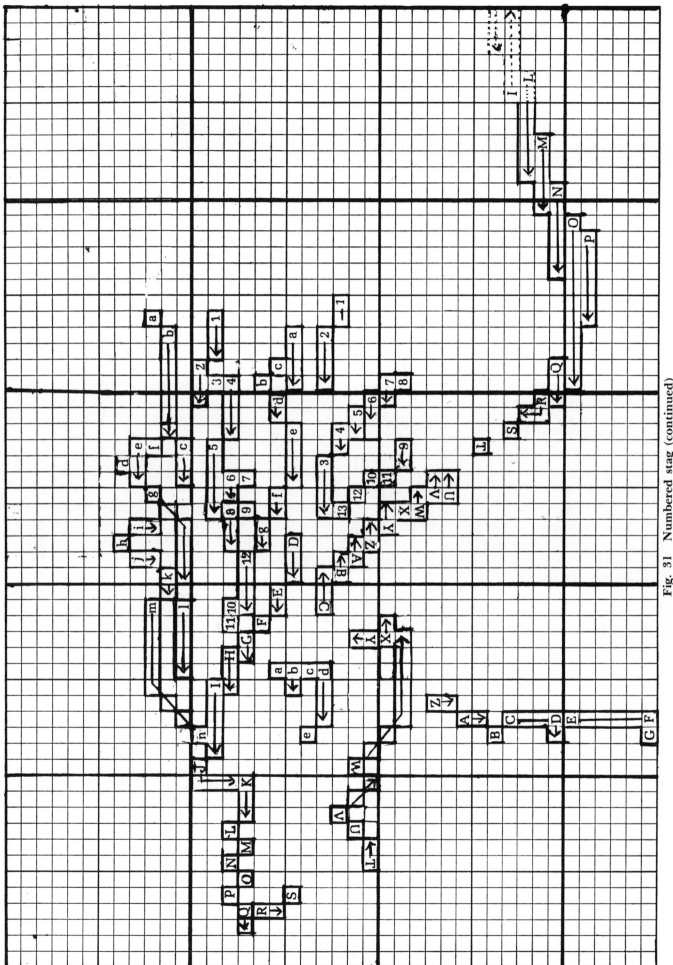

Fig. 31 Numbered stag (continued)

39
The Diagonal Dilemma

Because of the nature of the stitch, whether Continental, basket weave, or half cross-stitch, all of these slant like the accent aigu [/] diagonally over the intersection of the threads of the canvas (Fig. 32).

This creates an effect on the *progression* of the stitches. A 45-degree diagonal line of 45-degree stitches is naturally going to produce a clear-cut line if they are both traveling in the same direction upward from left to right (or downward from right to left).

When a diagonal is going in the opposite direction, upward from right to left (or downward from left to right), the direction of the diagonal is at *right angles* to the stitch. The stitches appear like steps.

Beginners are very puzzled by this. I saw a fellow customer in a book shop trying to find directions to avoid the problem.

I am afraid that even the most expert are stuck with this, so the only thing to do is look on it as an attractive and challenging feature.

To go up diagonally from lower left to upper right, turn the canvas upside down, unless you are left-handed.

There are ways you can make changes in the diagonal pattern. The two Mondrian details (Graph 48, a and b, Photograph 21, Plates XXVI, XXVII) are exactly the same design, but the placement on the canvas is different, creating a change in the effect of the diagonals. Plate XXVI was worked as a diamond shape and Plate XXVII as a square.

In Mr. Tod (Graph 49, Plate XXV), his shoulders and right cheeks are built on a pure diagonal. This adds style and simplicity to the design.

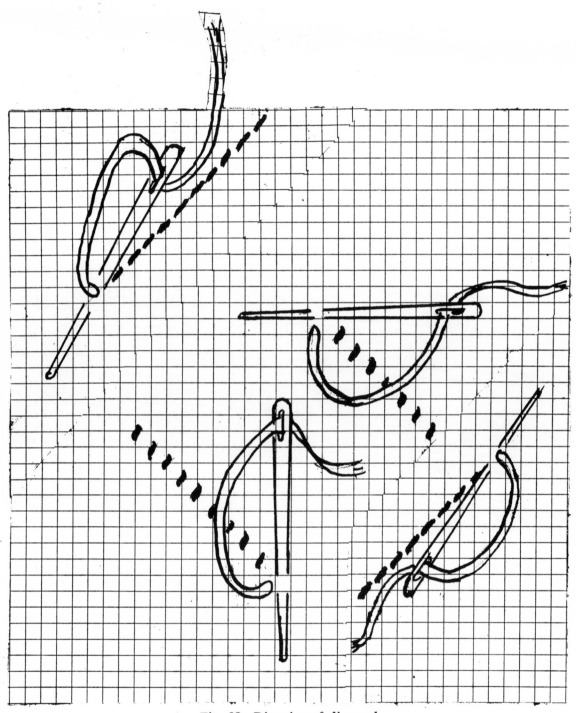

Fig. 32 Direction of diagonals

Graphs 48a and 48b Composition in Black and Gray on #10 graph. Adaptation from the painting by Piet Mondrian (Photograph 21, Plates XXVI, XXVII)

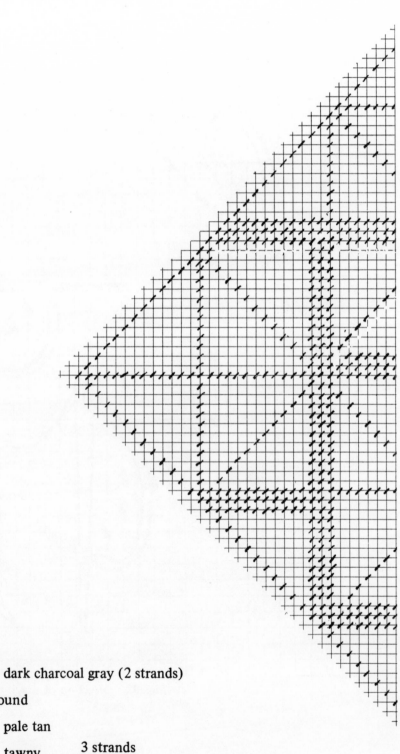

lines

162   dark charcoal gray (2 strands)

background

020   pale tan

025   tawny   3 strands
                    mixed

174   light toast

166

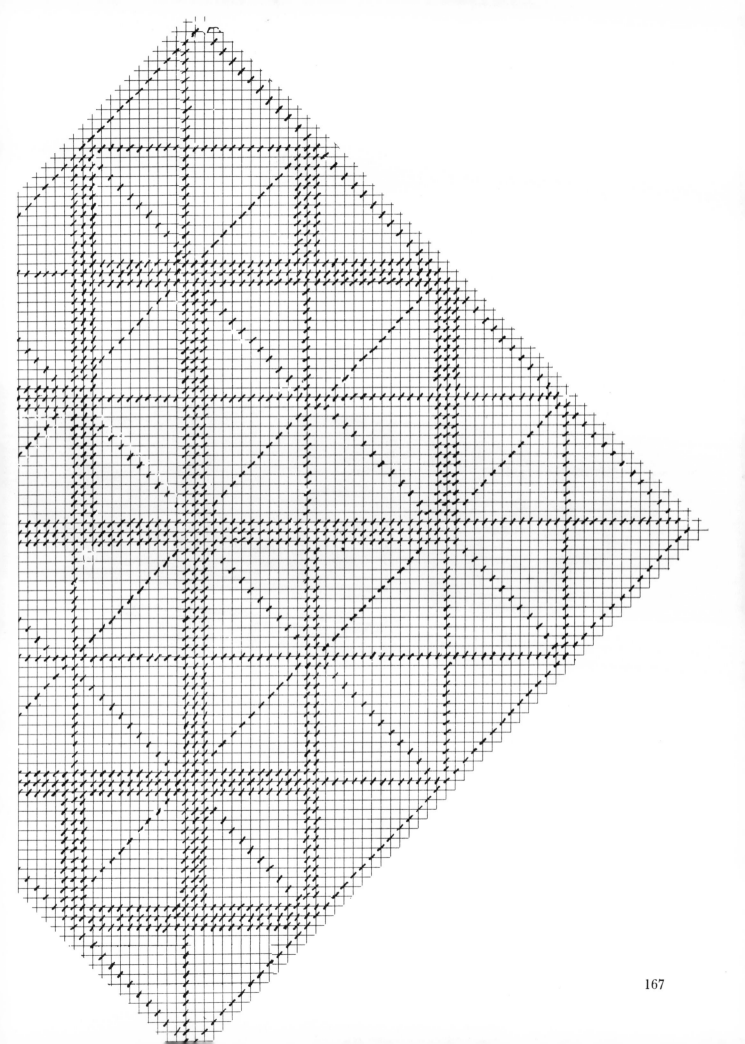

167

Photograph 21 Composition in Black and Gray. Piet
Mondrian, 1919. *The Philadelphia Museum of Art,
The Louise and Walter Arensberg Collection* (Graph
48, Plates XXVI and XXVII)

head, paws, vest, tail, buttons, legs

■	110	deep charcoal brown
◣	126	taupe
◢	267	deep venetian red
∧	414	deep brick
╱	416	brick
○	426	light brick
·	513	pale dill (eye outline and background)

collar, suit

■	504	deep forest green
◣	540	deep olive green
◢	504	deep forest green / 573 dill
∧	553	olive green
╱	573	dill
○	590	light olive green
·	563	light dill

Graph 49 Mr. Tod on #16 graph. Adaptation from
The Tale of Mr. Tod by Beatrix Potter (Plate XXV)

40
Your First Design

Here is an example of combining a little motif from the Metropolitan Museum (Fig. 33, top) with a geometric background. I am hoping you will go from this to your own museum finds and plan your own backgrounds. After you have studied all the various combinations in the book, it will become easier and more fun. Because this subject is small, it is better to fill the areas solidly, rather than outlining first, and with such an uneven shape the Continental is the best suited.

Start at A, on the head, having counted 6 holes up from the center [*], and then 7 stitches to the right. Work this row to the end of the arrow, then bring needle back underneath to B and work again to the left, skipping 2 holes for the eyes. Continue with C. On D work down 1 stitch vertically, a diagonal to the left, completing that row. (Keep alert for diagonals to follow.) Continue through E, F and G. Bring needle back underneath to H. On I turn canvas around for the 3 vertical stitches or use the AMBI-D stitch (see chapter 17, Left-Handed Needlepoint). Bring needle up underneath to J and work your way through M, going left on each row. DOWN at end of row and finish off yarn. Start again at N. After that row turn canvas and work back on O. Continue in this way, skipping 2 holes in rows O and P between the animal's chest and foot. Work down front foot, then the two back legs (Fig. 33, bottom).

For the diagonals, find a between e and h. Work the diagonal from a to b, b to c; turn canvas, work c to d and d to a.

Now fill 6 diagonal holes from each corner toward the center, and finally the 4 triangles.

Choose your own colors. The 4 triangles should be dark or bright to set off the diamond that encloses the animal. Last, work the background in white and pale colors.

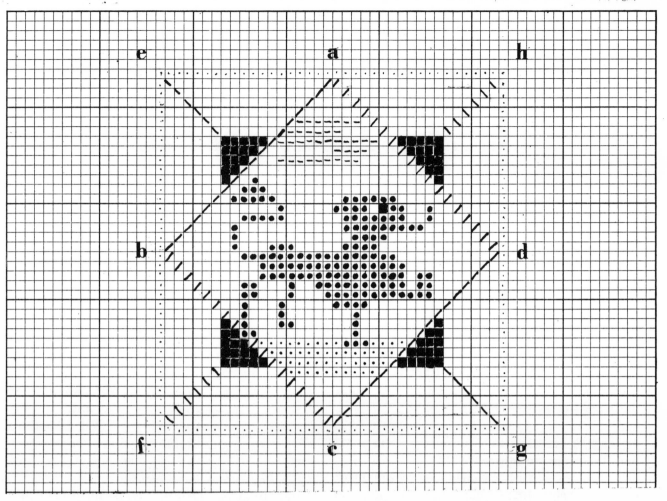

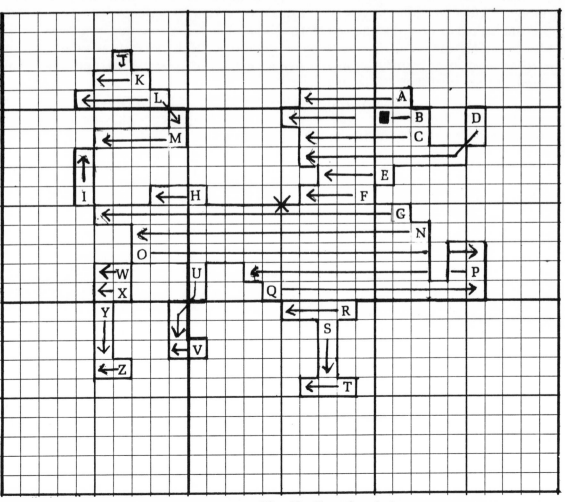

Fig. 33 Your first design

41
Blocking; Experiment Now

Tack some brown paper on a breadboard, drawing board, or any board larger than your final design. Draw a square in the center the same size as your finished canvas.

If the canvas is clean, simply sponge it from the back, a little at a time, until it is pliable and then lay it on the square.

If the canvas needs cleaning before you block it, slosh it gently up and down in a mild solution of water and Woolite. Rinse and squeeze gently. Washing removes the sizing, so don't be alarmed at how limp the canvas becomes.

Some prefer to have it cleaned professionally.

Take the damp canvas and lay it on the square. First tack the worked part of the canvas exactly over the penciled corners. Then work around the sides (Fig. 34), either shrinking or stretching as the case may be. (Use pushpins.)

When blocking a larger piece of work (or if it's soaking wet), allow several days for the canvas to dry.

When it is completely dry, apply rabbit-skin glue to the back. This comes only in powder form (see chapter 55, Materials). Heat in a double boiler 1 cup of water; slowly add 2 tablespoons of glue. When it is dissolved, remove from heat. It will cool into a custardlike mass. Use a spatula to spread the glue and subsequently scrape off the superfluous glue. This will give your canvas a good sizing so it will hold its shape.

Enough cannot be said about guarding against any disasters that might happen in blocking.

Sometimes the marker that you thought was permanent seems to bleed through the whites. (If it really is permanent it will disappear on drying.) The margin around the finished work that seemed adequate seems to ravel to nothing when wet. Even the limp quality can be upsetting, and a piece that has taken months to work seems in irrefutable jeopardy.

But by experimenting with small swatches, this nerve-racking experience can be avoided. Take some practice pieces that you have drawn and stitched on and block them carefully as if they were finished pieces. Then you will be assured that your marker *is* permanent and that wide 2-inch margins are important.

I hope no reader ever experiences the cold chill of realization that the worst has happened —the marking pen has bled through and one has the dreary choice of doing 40 hours or so of work again or painstakingly ripping out and attaching each loose piece of yarn securely before even beginning to rework the bared sections.

Since I wrote this chapter a new marking pen —NEPO— made by Sanford Corp. has come on the market. They explain: "Sometimes, during the blocking process, the ink which has been absorbed by the sizing in the canvas comes out with the sizing, staining the yarn." So-called waterproof markers are not formulated for this purpose. Something new had to be invented specifically for marking needlepoint canvas and NEPO is guaranteed for this.

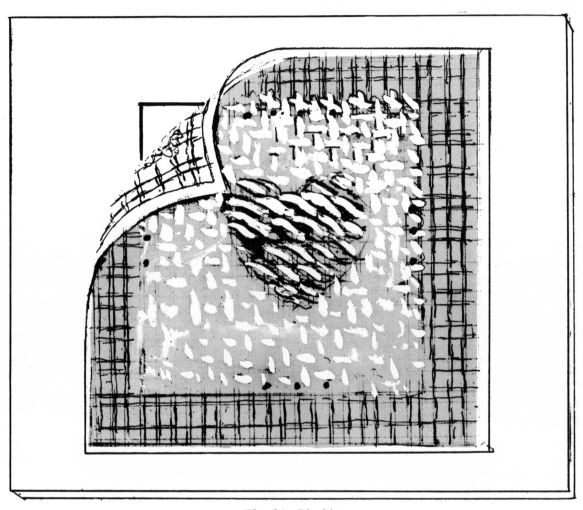

Fig. 34　Blocking

42
The Paternayan Brothers

The Paternayan Brothers in New York have the widest selection of colors and yarns in the world. Because they supply the smallest shops in the smallest towns as well as stores in large cities, I decided to pay them a visit.

When I walked into their shop, I stepped out of a dark, rainy day into a burst of colors as welcome as sunlight. During the few seconds' wait for Mr. Paternayan, I had an inspiration for an abstract design drawn completely from the random color relations of these yarns in their myriad pigeonholes.

My talk with Mr. Paternayan revealed that the family past was as colorful as their yarns. Arriving in America a half century ago, they set up shop mending Oriental rugs. This exacting work of course involved matching antique yarns and, in many cases, the needed colors were just not available. And so the Paternayans began to develop dyes—a complex and highly skilled art that does not permit any halfway measures. And today, because they have never permitted their own standards to waver, they continue to earn their high reputation.

43
Matching; by Yarn or by Number?

Yarns and canvases! This brings us to the subject of country and city buying. The difference in what and how you buy is considerable.

In the country you are expected to be professional and ask for the NUMBER of the yarn you desire (numbers are explained in chapter 55, Materials), like an artist who asks for ALIZARIN CRIMSON in an art store rather than bringing a color swatch to match.

The city salesgirl says it is quicker to take your yarn sample and run from pigeonhole to pigeonhole until she finds the desired match.

All shops, city and country, have Paternayan cards with identifying numbers on the sample yarns. I think it's important to have a looseleaf notebook and every time you buy a skein, Scotch Tape an inch or two of a strand in the book with the identifying number beside it. Have a separate page for each color family. Country stores are apt to have yarn in small hanks that are invaluable to store up.

Fashion in canvas is more prevalent in the city. Sometimes mono canvas is all that can be bought, so with every visit to the country, stock up on penelope in both white, which is best for painting designs on, and tan for following graphs because it's a more comfortable background, both on the eyes and because it doesn't show through as much as the white.

For hard-to-get canvas see chapter 55.

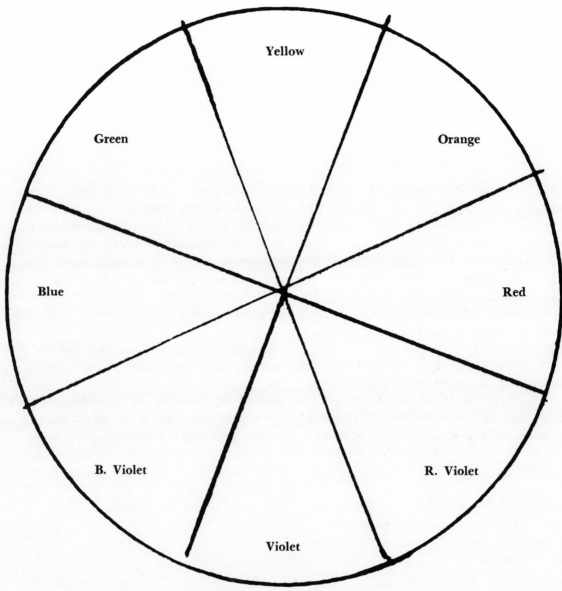

Fig. 35 Color spectrum

44
Color

I love color," cried a fellow purchaser as she gathered in her arms yellow, violet, red, and orange.

Color is a very personal matter. Some tend to like earth colors like ochre, umbers, grays, and the mustards and putty tones, and they use at most one or two bright colors in one design.

Others like the primary colors—red, yellow, and blue. But when experimenting with the secondary colors like green, orange, and blue violet and red violet, go easy.

Good advice is, unless you know what you are doing, go into color slowly. When viewing the yarns in pigeonholes in the shops, notice that each color comes in at least four shades. A design done on a white background using only four shades of blue, for example, can look finished and exciting.

Combining colors at opposite ends of the spectrum requires much more skill than using ones that are close together. Yellow or yellow orange set off with black will be far more pleasing than yellow and violet. In order to have the latter, it is necessary to work carefully down the spectrum, filling in between these two enemies (Fig. 35).

If you want to "shock" in the manner of the "pop" artists, then you must do as they do, get it across that you *are* shocking and don't get all the colors wrong unwittingly.

If you *must* have an orange pillow, then at least have the central motif in something like olive green and white.

Persian yarn for needlepoint has to be sold in one-ounce skeins, so it would be ideal to go to a shop with a friend or two and divide colors among you. Otherwise, start out with few colors and keep adding from time to time.

Sometimes it is possible to find Paternayan yarns in 4.2 gram amounts. Also, very small skeins of crewel yarns are a useful substitute for a small area.

45
What about Borders?

Borders can complement the central theme, or detract from it, and sometimes *no* border is the most effective of all.

For instance, Butterfly (Plate IV, Graph 50), in reaching out beyond the confines of the frame, dominates the space with such a feeling of expansion that a border would ruin the intent.

Coptic art, 1st- to 15th-century art of the Eastern Mediterranean, proved to be master of the border, with endless variations on scrolls, spirals, stylized leaf and tree shapes, vines, hearts, and abstract designs lending enchantment but taking second place to the main theme.

The American sampler border went to the other extreme, a phenomenon in extravagant borders often dipping dangerously into the main subject (Graph 51). They pursued their course florally around severe houses, the alphabet, or a weeping willow, acting as a complement to a stark central object.

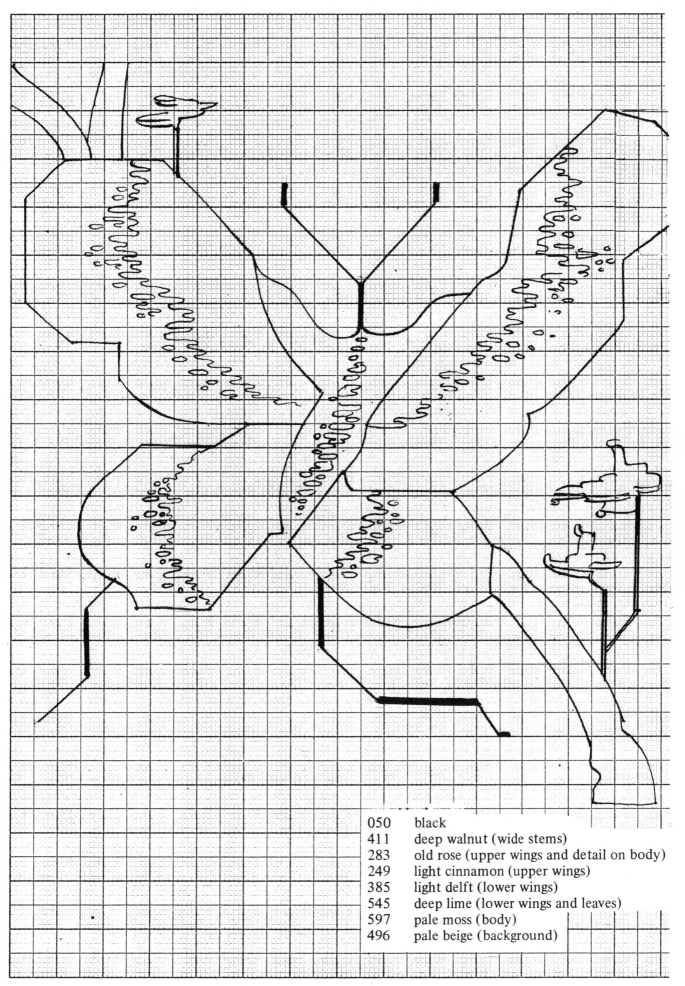

050	black
411	deep walnut (wide stems)
283	old rose (upper wings and detail on body)
249	light cinnamon (upper wings)
385	light delft (lower wings)
545	deep lime (lower wings and leaves)
597	pale moss (body)
496	pale beige (background)

Graph 50 Butterfly on #20 graph. (Plate IV)

Graph 51 Spiraling Border on #20 graph. Adaptation from *American Samplers* by Bolton and Coe (Dover Publications)

46
Personalize Your Design

In giving a present, initials or one letter not only gives a personal touch but can add style and interest.

Try superimposing letters over textile designs, for example.

Trace or make a Xerox copy of one of the letters in Graph 52 and place it on one of the textile pages, moving the letter around until you get an effect you like. Try not to have the letter in the middle.

Sometimes a pale letter over a strong textile is effective if there's a white stripe behind it to set it off, or over squares or stripes (Plates XII, XIII, XIV, XV).

After you have decided where you want the initial and what size canvas you will be using, transfer the initial directly onto the canvas, realizing that it will change in size according to the size of the canvas.

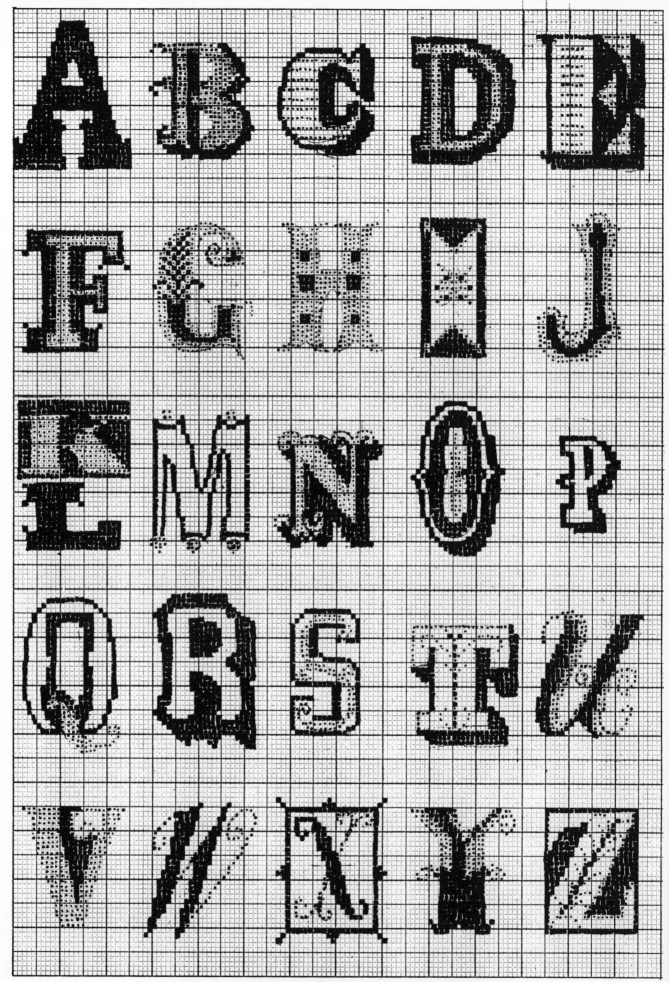

Graph 52 Initials on #20 graph. Adaptation of Old-Fashioned Type Specimens. *Robinson-Pforzheimer Collection. New York Public Library, fifth edition, 1969*

47
Design As You Go

Try marking off your canvas in horizontals, verticals, and diagonals.

Then design as you work, with only a general plan. You might draw some horizontals, verticals, and diagonals on the bare canvas. As you begin to fill in some of the lines and inner shapes, ideas will come to you about how you are to continue.

In an allover pattern (Plate XVIII) after it has been squared off you might think of a motif like the semicircles, then repeat them in each triangle. After that, add the horizontal brown lines. Finally, fill in each triangle as you please.

Photograph 22, "Geometric, Red and Pink," is also a design in which horizontals and verticals were drawn at random, then the large flat areas were filled in, first a stripe of one, then a solid block of the other, with the decision made in progress about the juxtaposition of the two tones. Finally the darkest areas were done, narrowing the rest down to smaller shades and shapes.

Photograph 22 Geometric, Red and Pink. 9 x 9 in. on #18 canvas. Designed and worked by Eleanor Hempstead

48
Mounting Pictures

Needlepoint pictures have a bad name, mostly because of poor composition and pretentious framing.

A needlepoint picture can dominate a small room in a most engaging way. In a hallway, study, anteroom, or guest room it is an intimate detail, a personal touch like a fresh bouquet.

Your picture should be planned to fit a standard stretcher (8", 10", 12", 14", and so on). *Sometimes* stretchers purchased at an art store come in ODD numbers, 9", 11", 13", and so on.

Stretchers are notched at each end. Assemble them by pushing two together at right angles. The tongue fits into the groove.

After you put your stretchers together they must be perfectly square, like any frame.

A square is the obvious means of checking the corners, but putting it against a door jamb is an excellent substitute.

Sometimes the door jamb isn't true (Fig. 36a) but as long as the relationship of the door jamb to the stretcher frame is consistent as you turn it, it will be all right. Keep tapping corners with a hammer until the stretchers are square.

Always tap at the *lower* corner. Turn stretcher upside down to do this, if necessary.

Sponge the canvas lightly with water as for blocking. Don't soak unless absolutely necessary.

The more experienced you become, the more care you will take to avoid major blocking by trying to keep your canvas square and clean as you work it, because stretching a soaking-wet canvas is more difficult than blocking it on a flat board. Sometimes it takes hours to line up and wrestle with the out-of-shape canvas that pulls against you with the wet stitches literally squeezing the canvas out of shape.

Instead of tacking the corners of the canvas first, as in blocking, use thumb tacks or push pins and start at the center of each stretcher, working toward each corner. When you are satisfied that each corner is correct and the stitched edges are flush with the stretcher edges, fold back the raw canvas over the wood and tack (Fig. 36b).

Start replacing the thumbtacks with tacks or staples, beginning in the center of a side. Then tack or staple the opposite side, and so on. Keep on pulling the canvas as you go to make it taut. Remember, you will always be pulling at opposite sides. See Figure 36c and d, for dealing with the corners.

After the canvas is "squared" and "stretched" and if it is at all slack, triangles called "keys" are provided for hammering into the corners, where you will notice small slots. Give each key the same number of short firm knocks as you turn the canvas around.

Now you are ready to frame. Lumber yards carry lattice 1/4" by 11/2" or 13/4" wide.

With a fine saw and a square (see chapter 55) saw four pieces 1" longer than each side of the stretcher.

Hammer 11/2" brads in each piece every 3 or

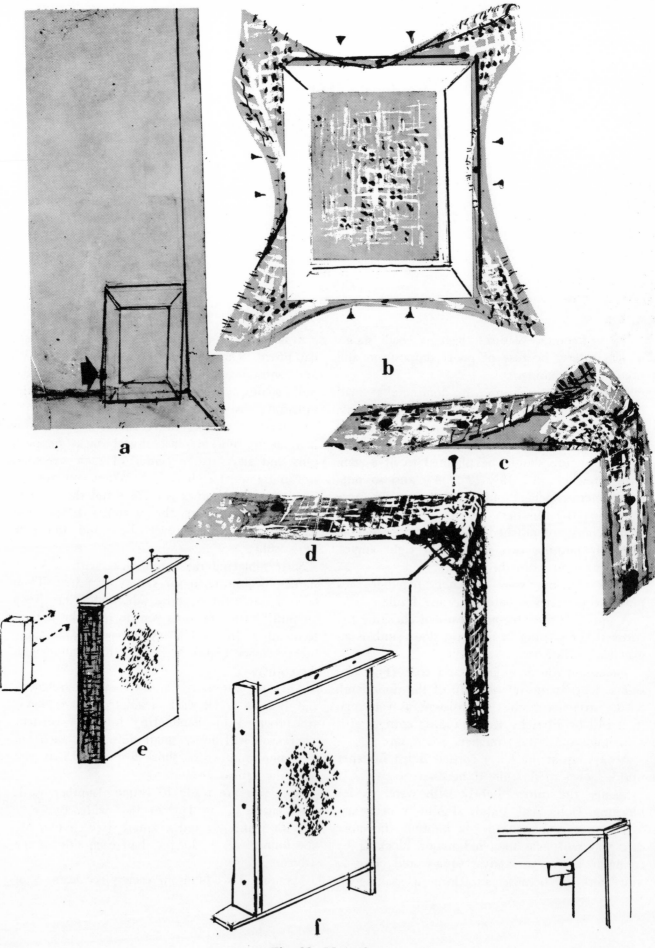

Fig. 36 Mounting

4 inches, having made a small hole with an awl first.

Place one piece of lattice along an edge; see that one edge is flush with the front of the canvas (Fig. 36e).

Square up the first corner against a flat surface. A block of wood works well.

After hammering in the first slat, turn canvas once and push slat No. 2 firmly against the protruding inch of slat No. 1. Continue until the four slats are nailed on.

Hammer ½" brads into the corners, saw off protruding ends, and sand corners to round them slightly (Fig. 36f). Leave wood plain, or rub on a mahogany or walnut stain with a cloth.

49
Chinese Motifs

Zebra, Geranium, and Chinese Motifs— these three designs all have different approaches. Zebra (Plate XXVIII), once the general idea was established, became a spontaneous play between light and dark. The Geranium (Plate XXIX) is a fresh design, and once the petals and leaves were established, it was simply a matter of carrying it out. Then a pleasant time was spent without worries filling in the background.

Chinese Motifs (Plate XXX) is complex by comparison. Here is a description of how it is done.

Plan for the fretwork and one octagon (Fig. 37, Plate XXX, Graphs 53, 54).

Put in the single-stitch background first, and then fill in the 2-stitch-wide fretwork in basket weave.

The background for the fretwork starts with a 25-stitch upright with a 19-stitch crossbar at each end, and at right angles to this, from the 4th stitch from either end, a 3-stitch branch parallel to the upright. The same motif appears again, with the 19-stitch crossbars vertical and the 25-stitch members horizontal.

The octagons are placed at random and stitched in first, and then the orange fretwork background is started at one end and completely finished before filling in the octagons.

This makes it easier to pick up the fretwork background where it has been interrupted by an octagon (or any other suitable shape).

Two shades of wool, olive green and light yellow, are used, each separately and also a thread of each together at random, giving an effect of weaving and age. These are the same two colors used in the designs in the octagons, with occasionally a brighter yellow for accent.

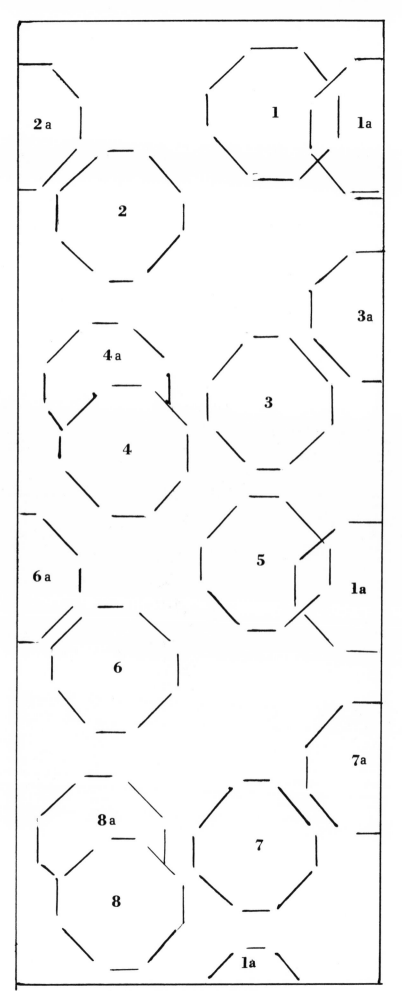

Fig. 37   Chinese Motifs

189

	958	orange red	Fretwork and background of medallions
	573	dill	} background between fretwork
	541	pale olive	
	573	dill	
	541	pale olive	} motifs
	580	pale lime	

Graph 53 Chinese Motifs on #20 graph (Plate XXX)

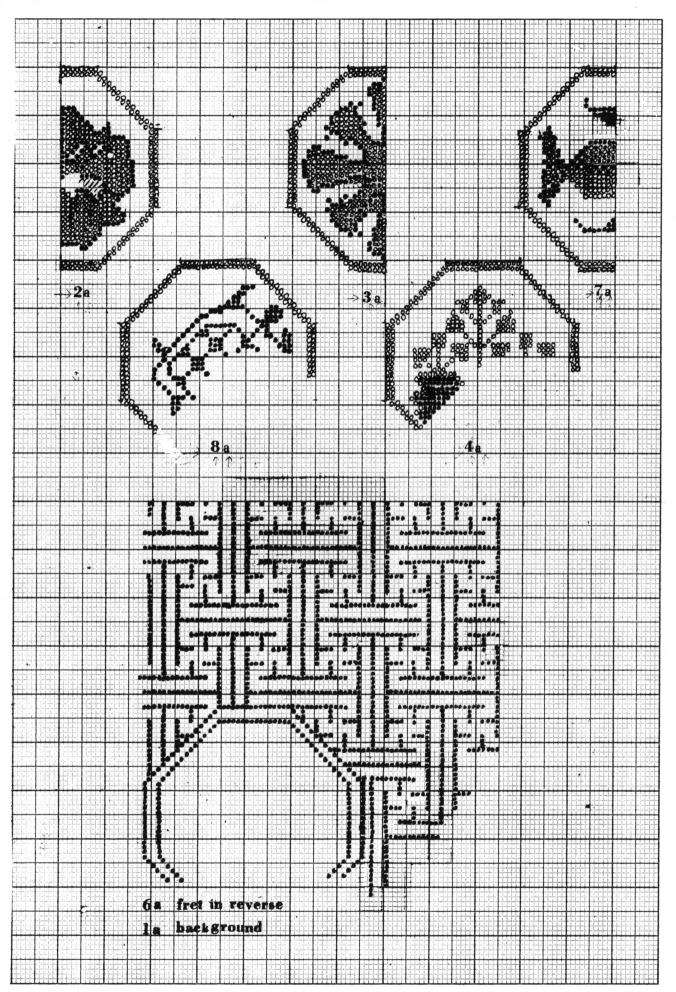

Graph 54 Chinese Motifs on #20 graph (Plate XXX)

50
The Tailored Look

An overall rule in making small things (eyeglass cases, belts, etc.) is to go easy on the edging and binding. Otherwise they are apt to be clumsy and confining, and, in the case of eyeglass cases, a cording can be overpowering for something so small.

An eyeglass case done in petit point light enough to be lined, turned, French seamed where it remains open and top-stitched where the sides come together, comes out trim and tailored (Fig. 38).

Besides Persian yarn, try mouliné, an embroidery silk that makes a nice, sleek, needlepoint stitch.

Pillows to be inserted in your pillow cover can be bought in various sizes, but if you make your own, stuffing them with kapok, you can make them any size you wish.

To make the inside pillow, seam muslin or a sheeting material, leaving the last side open. Turn right side out and slip stitch the last edges after stuffing.

Needlepoint pillow and pincushion linings can be made out of velvet, wool, corduroy, silk, etcetera. Be sure that the color is a good complement to your design.

A pillow is large enough to hold its own with cording, but think twice before adding tassels (Fig. 39).

Coasters, like pillows, are stitched on three sides and stuffed with either several layers of in-terfacing or thin cork or cardboard. The last two look nicer but of course are not washable. After the coaster is filled, the fourth side is slip-stitched.

A rug is made on the same theory but should not be attempted until you have mastered smaller things. A suitable backing for a rug is heavy linen (Fig. 39).

Study Guéridon (Fig. 40, Photograph 23, Graph 55), Kunterbunt (Graph 56), and Matrose (Graph 57), three masterpieces that would make excellent rugs.

Belts can be made straight or curved. For the latter, trace a contour belt on brown paper or shelf paper, making it the length of your waist measurement. (The amount taken up by the buckle will compensate for the extra length needed to lap over the buckle.) Save the tracing to use as a guide for the blocking.

Trim the tracing down to the outline and lay it on #10 point canvas. After drawing around the pattern, make a 2″ margin around this. In working the belt design (Photograph 24, Graph 58) be sure that the heads are equidistant from the two ends and space the other heads accordingly. After working the belt, you can fill in the outside curves with petit point to assure a smoother seam.

Follow Figure 41 for finishing, lining it with taffeta or anything else that holds its shape.

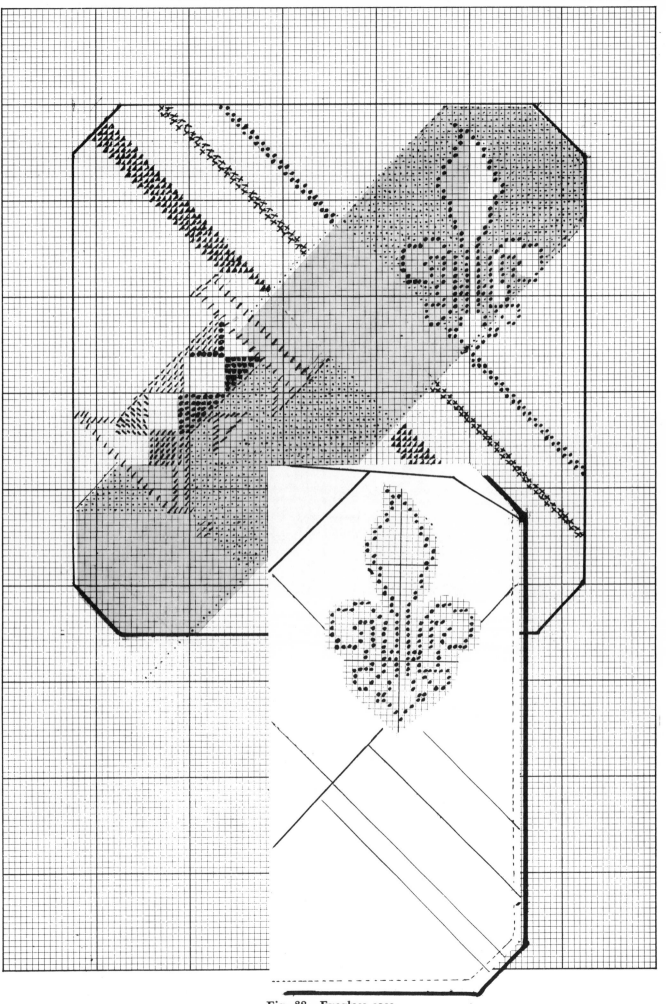

Fig. 38 Eyeglass case

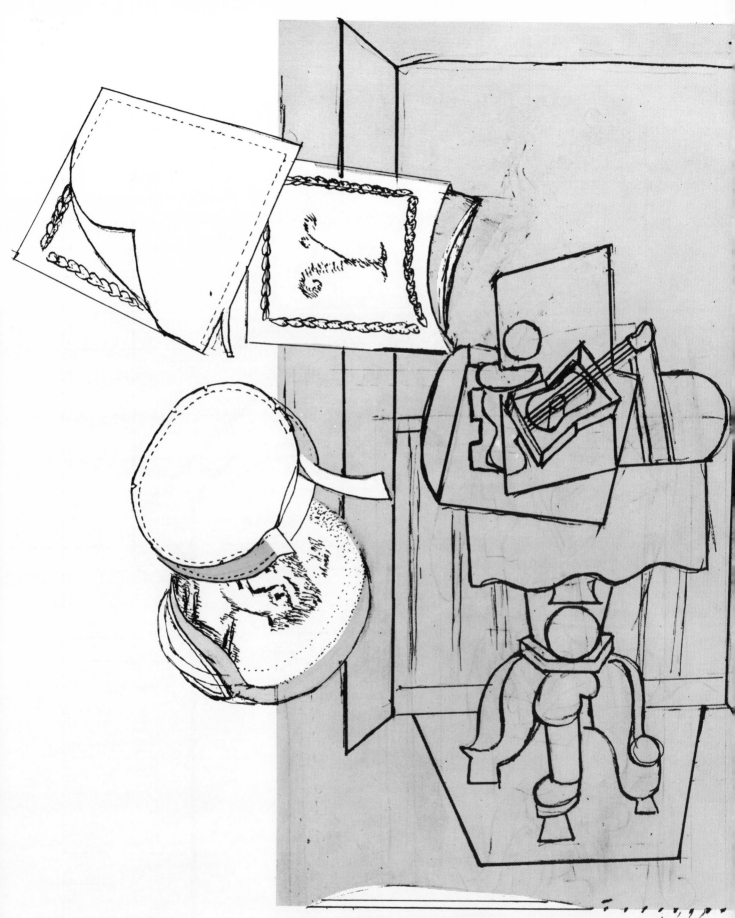

Fig. 39   Pillows and rug

Photograph 23 Guéridon. Crayon, Picasso, 1920.
Galerie Louise Leiris, Paris (Graph 55, Fig. 40)

Fig. 40 Photostat of Guéridon, photograph

Graph 55 Guéridon on #20 graph. Adaptation from
the drawing by Picasso (Photograph 23, Fig. 40)

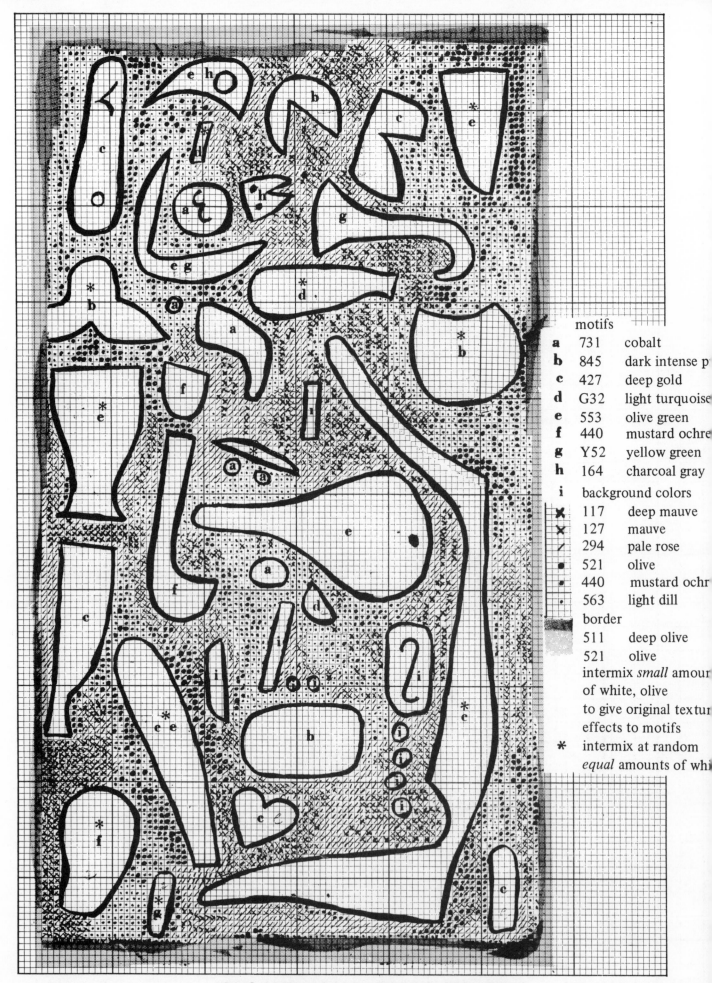

motifs

a	731	cobalt
b	845	dark intense p...
c	427	deep gold
d	G32	light turquoise
e	553	olive green
f	440	mustard ochre...
g	Y52	yellow green
h	164	charcoal gray
i	background colors

✕	117	deep mauve
✕	127	mauve
╱	294	pale rose
▪	521	olive
▫	440	mustard ochr...
·	563	light dill

border

511	deep olive
521	olive

intermix *small* amoun...
of white, olive
to give original textur...
effects to motifs

✱ intermix at random
equal amounts of whi...

Graph 56 Kunterbunt on #16 graph. Adaptation of
Kunterbunt by Paul Klee. *Collection Gallerie Beyeler,
Basle, Switzerland*

a 741 pale cobalt
b 731 cobalt
c 162 dark charcoal gray
d 133 light cocoa
e 553 olive green
f 550 lime $\}$ mixed
g 531 light olive $\}$ at random
* 531 intermix small amounts
of light olive with all
colors other than blues

b$\}$
c$\}$ 731 and 162 mixed at random

■ 050 black (lines)

Graph 57 Matrose on #20 graph. Adaptation of Matrose by Paul Klee. *Collection of Mrs. Victor Babin,
Cleveland, Ohio*

Photograph 24 Border of Heads. Coptic, Fifth to Sixth Century A.D. The Brooklyn Museum, Charles Edwin Wilbour Fund (Graph 58)

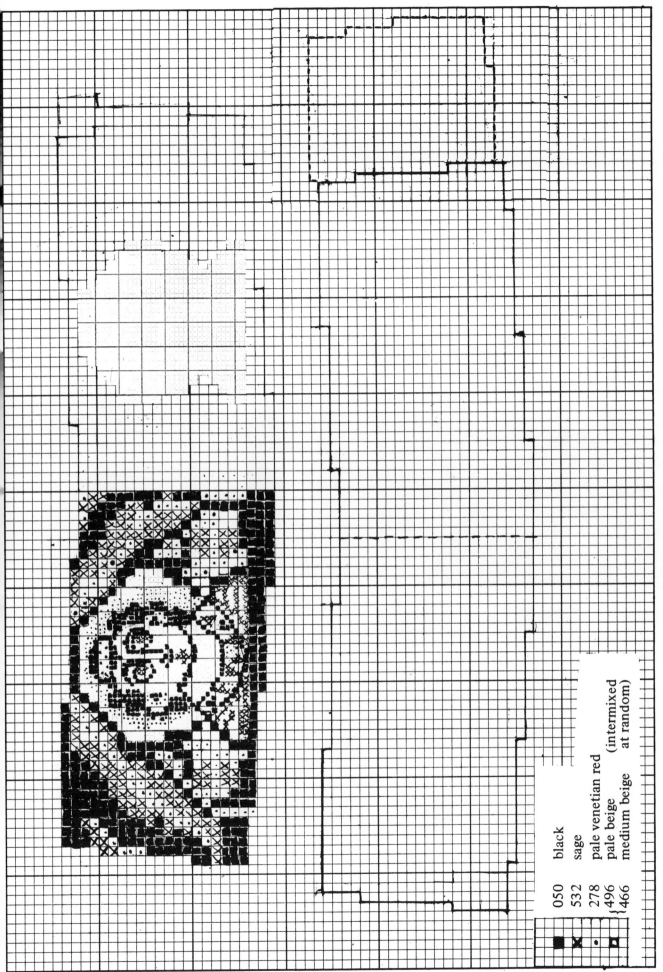

■	⊠	·	▫

050   black
532   sage
278   pale venetian red
{496   pale beige   (intermixed
{466   medium beige   at random)

Graph 58 Border of Heads on #10/20 graph. Adaptation of a Coptic textile (Photograph 24)

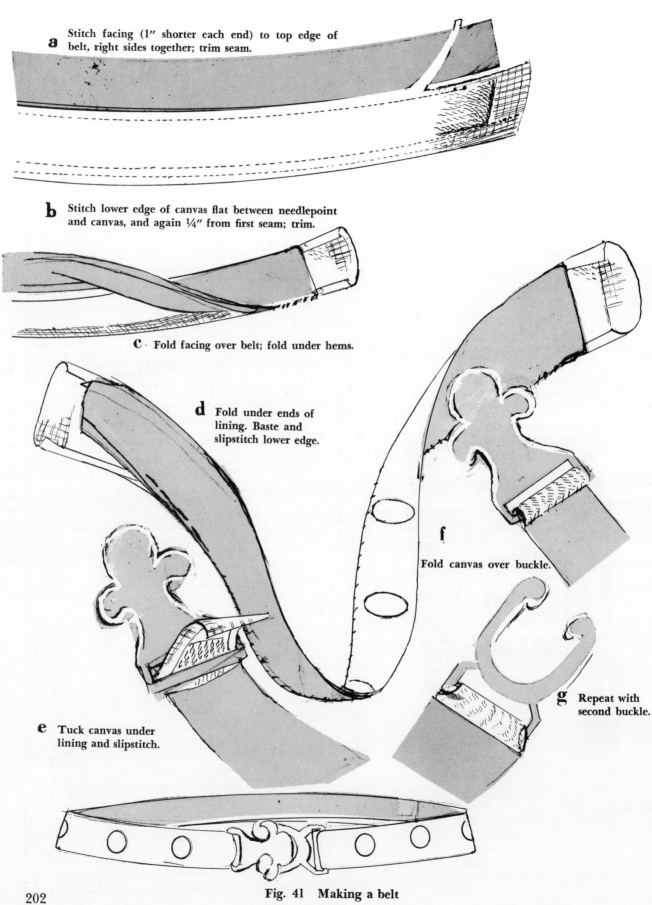

a Stitch facing (1″ shorter each end) to top edge of belt, right sides together; trim seam.

b Stitch lower edge of canvas flat between needlepoint and canvas, and again ¼″ from first seam; trim.

c Fold facing over belt; fold under hems.

d Fold under ends of lining. Baste and slipstitch lower edge.

f Fold canvas over buckle.

g Repeat with second buckle.

e Tuck canvas under lining and slipstitch.

Fig. 41 Making a belt

51
Notes on the Graph Drawings

Graph drawings are an excellent way of giving you ideas about the possibilities of museum motifs as seen through a needlepointer's eyes, and about how a design, by enlarging, simplifying, isolating, or adding, takes on another dimension. For instance, a pillow with a Coptic face (Graph 26) becomes a different thing from what it was on a museum wall. Humor and a feeling of today move in to complement a traditional surrounding.

As you look through the graph drawings, try to think of interesting relationships: A sampler bird and flower on a background of diagonal stripes, squares, diamond shapes, or plain with a border or a series of borders. Allover patterns like the "cane" or "Greek key" (Graphs 8, 14) relieved by a band of white or plain color would make a good background for an initial or flower (Graphs 10, 52, 63).

In the case of the carousel rabbit (Graph 13, Plates Xa and Xb), you might like a bright red saddle, yellow collar, and so on. Many of the designs are shaded only, leaving the color variations up to you.

If you live in the country or a village, here is a project for you—an old house (Graph 59, Plate XXXI) or a map landscape (Plate XXXII) of the town's historical sites and geographic characteristics.

In most of the graph illustrations there is a key beside the symbols with a number that refers to the Paternayan color chart found in most needlepoint shops throughout the country.

Not all shops carry a complete supply of all the shades so in some cases substitutes will have to be made. All colors are divided into "families." For instance, deep indigo ranging to pale indigo is all the same *color* in different *shades*.

Of course, you can use colors to suit your taste, particularly with animals, birds, and background. In the paintings, stay with the colors designated, which are as close as possible to the originals.

In regular size canvas #14 to #5, where two or more threads are used, a mixture of shades can be worked at the same time. In petit point only one thread will fit into a hole at a time and so the stitches must be worked at random—first one shade and then another until you reach the desired result.

Most of the paintings would make excellent rugs. A #20 graph illustration worked on #5 canvas would be four times the size of the graph drawing. If you prefer a rug on #10 canvas, read how to enlarge by squaring off in chapter 26, Sequence of a Zinnia.

Many designs have areas with no symbols in either the foreground or the background. These may be white or in the color of your choice, but both should be the same color. (See chapter 18, From Rabbits to Rectangles.)

At times there may be variations between the finished needlepoint and the graph illustrations. Don't worry about it.

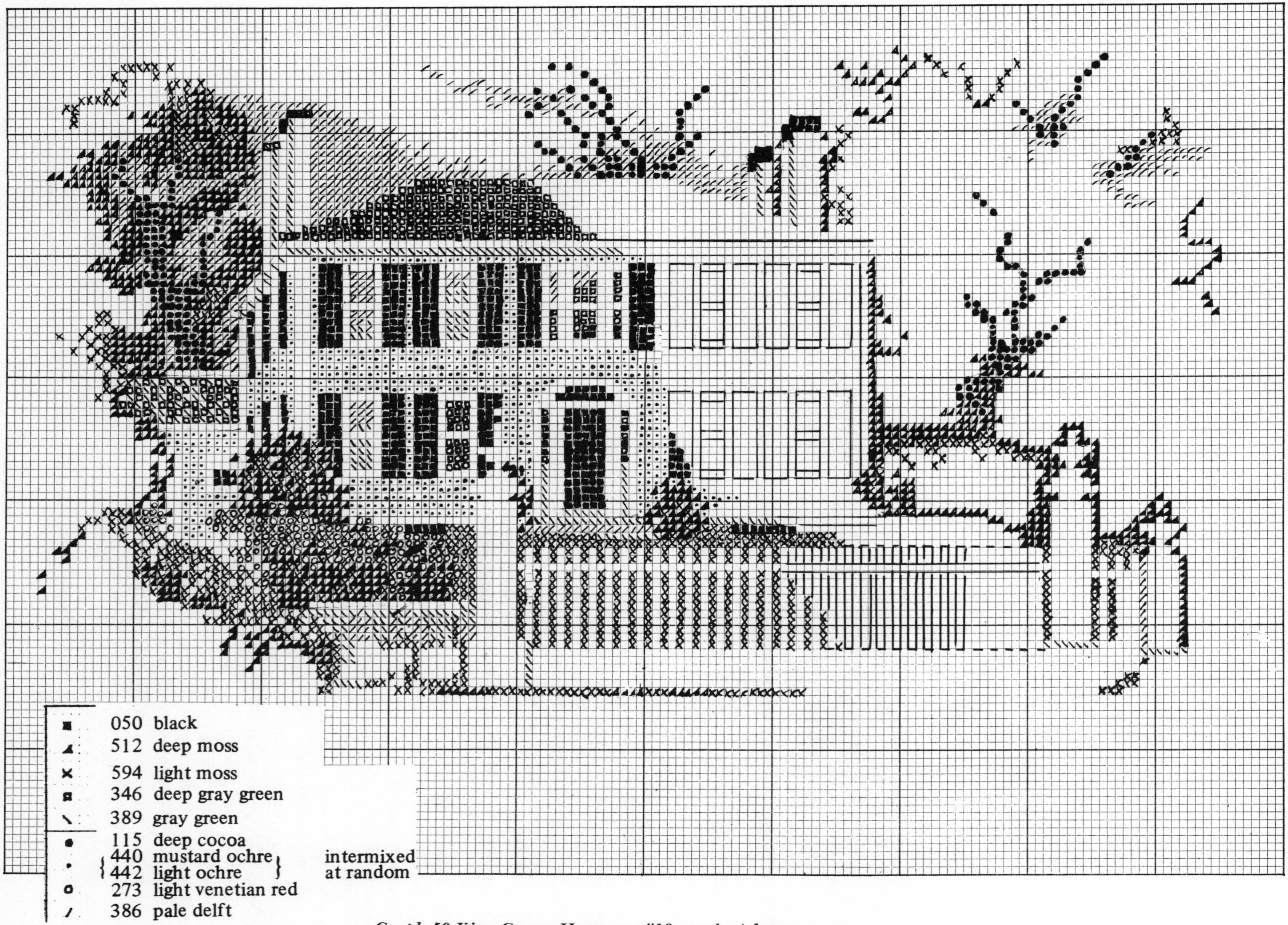

Graph 59 King Caesar House on #16 graph. Adapta-

■	050	black
◢	512	deep moss
✕	594	light moss
▣	346	deep gray green
╱	389	gray green
●	115	deep cocoa
·	{440	mustard ochre }
	{442	light ochre }
○	273	light venetian red
╱	386	pale delft

intermixed
at random

52
Notes at Random

In trying to cover every question that might arise, it might appear that there are more rules than necessary. Feel free to carry out a design technically in the way that suits you best. Mr. Tod (Graph 49, Plate XXV), for example, was developed from just a few pencil lines on the canvas. In writing a book it is necessary to run the gamut, showing the simplest to the most elaborate means. Then there is a range to suit all readers.

Don't be alarmed by too many suggestions for materials. At first try substitutes to discover the advantages of certain equipment.

For instance, there are two simple ways to trace from photographs and reproductions. One is to place the picture on a window pane, with a piece of tracing graph paper on top, and draw the outlines and shade with a soft pencil. Remove and carefully fill in squares with light, medium, and dark, either in a color or grays and black. The second is a homemade light table. If you use this method you can trace the squares directly. A piece of plexi-glass or a pane of glass is laid on a pile of books with a Tensor light underneath. See chapter 36, Don't Be Afraid of Being a Pro, for details about a light table.

Don't be upset if you have no graph paper with the same number of squares to the inch as the canvas you plan to work. For instance, if you are planning on a 10 square to the inch and have only 5 square to the inch graph, use it, realizing that the design will come out twice as large. In fact, large graph is easier to use in blocking out color.

Some prefer working on a pure canvas and so count off the squares on the designed graph paper. Others would rather trace right onto the canvas. Either way is valid.

In an adaptation of a motif, do what is natural to you. In the case of a flower, for instance, look for your own pattern or rhythm to accent.

Here are some flowers that are tracings from photographs. The Pansy (Graph 60) was traced three times in line and mass and placed against a textile background.

The Azalea was a more ambitious adaptation from a flower catalogue. First a photostat (Fig. 42) was made, was blown up to the size of this page, and then #10 graph paper was superimposed (Graph 61) and the shading roughly blocked in. Then the drawing was removed and the gray tone and symbols were placed.

Keep yarn away from scissors and canvas. If you don't, the yarn will soon acquire a fuzzy look.

See chapter 55, Materials for canvas and graph paper sizes.

Another way of numbering the canvas than

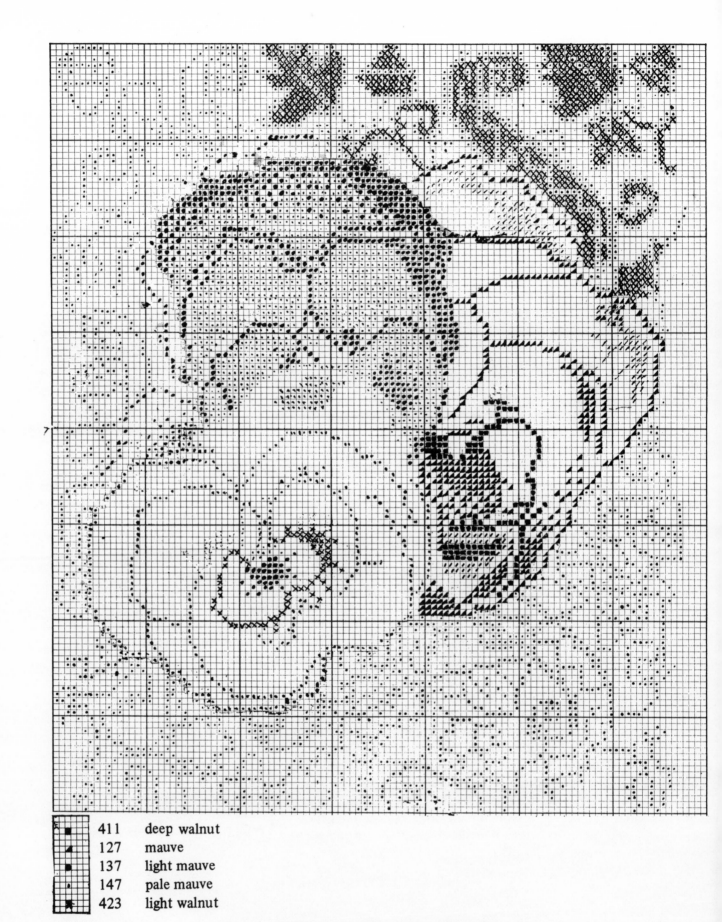

	411	deep walnut
	127	mauve
	137	light mauve
	147	pale mauve
	423	light walnut

Graph 60 **Pansies on #16 graph. Adaptation of a pansy from a catalogue**

206

Fig. 42 Photostat of azaleas in Wayside catalogue

	512	deep moss		855	intense pink		182	gray
	594	light moss		865	pale pink		184	light gray
	960	deep orange	{	865	pale pink		186	pale gray
			{	005	white			
	Y42	carat gold	{	186	pale gray	{	186	pale gray
			{	005	white	{	865	pale pink
	005	white (flower)		865	pale pink (background)			

that used in Figure 26 is to use the map system, with letters running horizontally on the top border and numbers running down the side border. This eliminates actual numbers on the canvas but is somewhat slower for finding the desired square.

On the worksheet you have made from Figure 26, letter above the top squares A–G and number down the side border 1–10. Now you can see, for instance, that square 21 is G3 (Fig. 44).

Graph 61 Azaleas on #10 graph. Adaptation from catalogue of The Wayside Gardens Co., Mentor, Ohio (Fig. 42)

53
The Sequence of a Photostat

Quite a bit easier than enlarging by hand is the use of the photostat and it is less expensive than the regular photograph (see chapter 34, Enlarging—Photostat, Lucida).

A photostat can never be blown up more than double its size at a time. This necessitates steps alternating between negative and positive prints to reach the desired dimension.

Whereas Figure 4 (chapter 3, Mono and Penelope), double the size of the original post card, has been enlarged only once to a matte negative, Figure 43a and b has alternated through four steps from negative to positive to reach a size seven times that of the original.

A glossy negative, though higher in price, produces more clarity of detail than matte (see chapter 55, Materials). Sometimes a matte *positive* is useful when it is necessary to change and draw on the print.

To enlarge Roundel (Photograph 25, Graph 62) have the "pie" shape blown up to any size you wish. Laying the photostat on a light table or against a window pane, right side down, trace the lines that will show through the back of the photostat. This is your reverse tracing that mirrors sections 1 and 4 (see detail, Fig. 45). Now you are ready to trace all the lines onto your canvas. After you have completed section 1, turn the photostat over and trace section 2 from the back side. After you have finished sections 3 and 4 in the same manner, you will have a circle twice the size of your photostat.

Because of the limited space, only the center of Roundel was used to show the steps in enlarging a photostat. If you double the size of Roundel, the circle would be approximately 12″ in diameter; if you quadruple it, the motif would be approximately 24″.

Photograph 25 Roundel. Coptic, Third to Fourth
Century A.D. *The Metropolitan Museum of Art, Purchase Subscription Fund* (Graph 62)

1. ORIGINAL   4. NEGATIVE
2. NEGATIVE   5. POSITIVE
3. POSITIVE

Each step is twice the size of the one before except for No. 5, which is the same size as its preceding negative, No. 4.

Fig. 43a   Sequence of the photostat

212

Fig. 43b   Sequence of the photostat (continued)

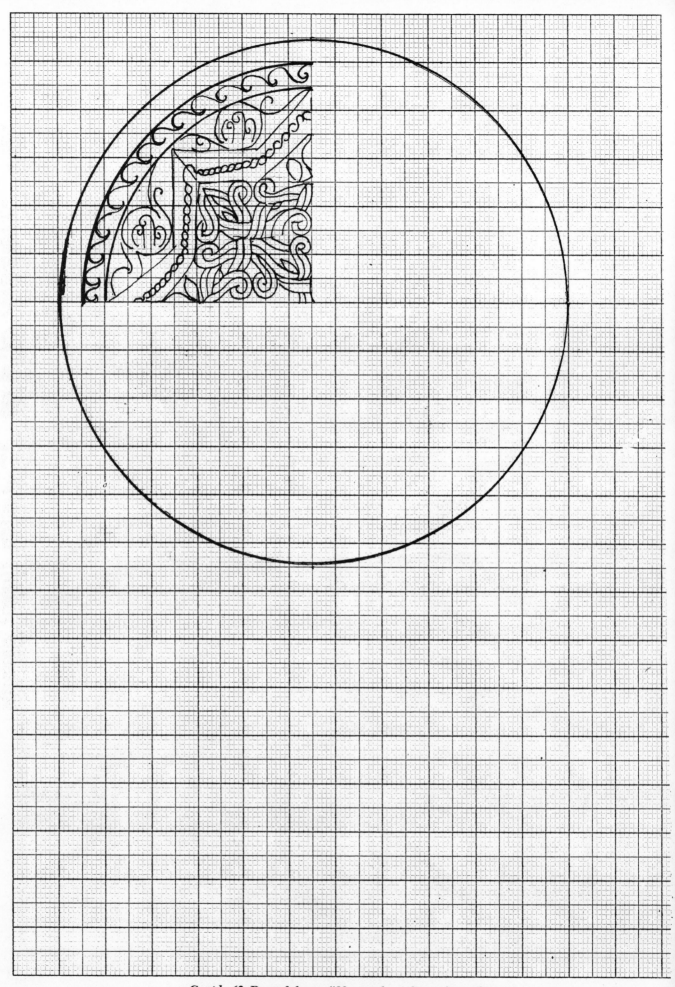

Graph 62 Roundel on #20 graph. Adaptation of a
Coptic textile (Photograph 25, Figs. 43a and b, 45)

	A	B	C	D	E	F	G	
	1	2	3	4	5	6	7	1
	8	9	10	11	12	13	14	2
	15	16	17	18	19	20	21	3
	22	23	24	25	26	27	28	4
	29	30	31	32	33	34	35	5
	36	37	38	39	40	41	42	6
	43	44	45	46	47	48	49	7
	50	51	52	53	54	55	56	8
	57	58	59	60	61	62	63	9
	64	65	66	67	68	69	70	10

Fig. 44 Canvas gauge, another work sheet

Fig. 45   Detail for sequence of the photostat

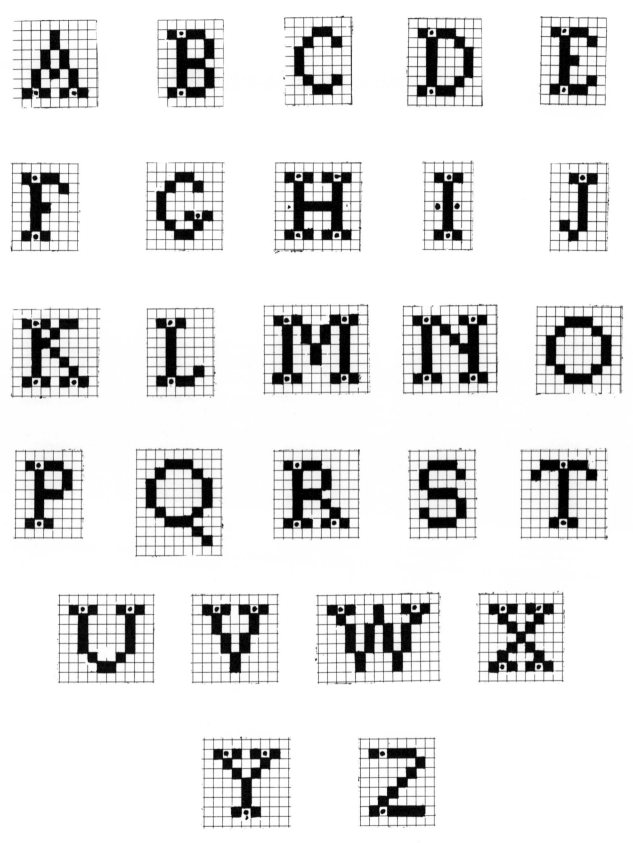

Graph 63 The Alphabet on #10 graph

54
Necessary Equipment

For Working the Canvas

Canvas, yarns, assorted needles, shears, embroidery scissors, and ripper, thimble, pincushion with needle sharpener, a bag with pockets to hold your work, plastic bags with "twistems" for the yarn you are using, plastic boxes that fit one over the other for storage, and masking tape.

For Designing

NEPO waterproof marker (light, medium, and dark), a heavy black marking pen or India ink and drawing pen for drawing the design so it will show through the canvas, tracing and graph paper (some 5 & 10 cent stores carry graph loose and in composition books).

For a wider selection of graph paper, look in the yellow pages for architect supplies.

A selection of fine-point ball points is invaluable for sketching and filling in the graph squares when planning a design.

Brown paper in large sheets, useful for patterns and large sketches, can be purchased in hardware stores.

Light table or a substitute.

Compass.

Most towns and cities now have shops that sell needlepoint supplies. The following list deals mostly with New York City. It includes a number of stores that sell by mail order and will be useful to people who cannot find local suppliers.

Most stores are willing to fill any orders, large or small. Some have a price list. With any inquiry, always send a stamped self-addressed envelope.

Country stores have room for an assortment of belt buckles, bag handles, and pillows of varying sizes to be stuffed into needlepoint covers.

Most shops sell needlepoint books and have arrangements for having their customers' work made up into pillows, eyeglass cases, bags, and so on.

BOUTIQUE MARGO, 26 W. 54 St., New York City 10019

See chart for canvas price list showing the variety of canvases there are. "Antique" on the chart is referred to as "ecru" in the text of this book.

NEEDLEPOINT CANVAS (French, Swiss)

Mono (single mesh)
Uni Superior white . . . .
"   "   " . . . .
"   "   " . . . .
"   "   antique . . . .
"   "   white . . . .
"   "   antique . . . .
"   "   white . . . .
"   "   antique . . . .

Toile Colbert, flesh . . . .
"   "   "
Silk Petit Point Canvas, cream . . . .
"   "   "   "   "

Penelope (double mesh)
rug, white, heavy quality . . . .
rug, antique, heavy quality . . . .
white, light quality . . . .
"   "   " . . . .
"   "   " . . . .
"   heavy quality . . . .
antique, heavy quality . . . .
white, light quality . . . .

cross-stitch, blue lines . . . .
"   "   "   " . . . .
"   "   "   " . . . .

size	width	price
10 mesh	40 inches	$ 9.00 yd
12 "	37 "	8.00
14 "	36 "	8.00
14 "	36 "	8.00
16 "	36 "	7.00
16 "	36 "	7.00
18 "	36 "	7.00
18 "	36 "	7.00
18 "	24 "	7.00
24 "	24 "	7.00
29 "	40 "	25.00
38 "	40 "	25.00
5/10 "	40 "	8.50
7/14 "	36 "	8.00
8/16 "	22 "	4.00
9/18 "	36 "	7.50
10/20 "	39 "	8.00

10/20	"	36	"	6.50
10/20	"	35	"	5.50
12/24	"	24	"	4.50
8/16	"	27	"	3.00
14/28	"	27	"	3.50
16/32	"	27	"	3.50

SELMA'S ART NEEDLEWORK, 1645 Second Avenue, New York City 10028.

ALICE MAYNARD, 724 Fifth Avenue, New York City 10022

The usual supplies, with an unusually large selection of yarns.

Some other needlepoint shops in New York are NINA NEEDLEPOINT, 860 Madison Ave., 10021; MAZALTOV'S, INC., 758 Madison Ave., 10021; WOOLWORK'S, INC., 783 Madison Ave., 10021.

NEEDLECRAFT HOUSE, West Townsend, Mass. 01474 (Lockweave canvas sold here.)

THE YARNERY, Rindge Center, New Hampshire, 03461

Belt buckle in Figure 41 from The Yarnery

ELLY, P.O.B. 3898, New Haven, Connecticut, 06525

Needlepointers' mesh and stitch count identifier. Matching grid tells count per inch.

This gadget ($2.00 plus postage) is very useful for a quick identification of how many squares to the inch in your canvas.

NEEDLEWOMAN'S SHOP, Duxbury, Massachusetts 02332

NEEDLES AND PINS, Peterboro Plaza, Peterborough, New Hampshire 03458

These shops carry a selection of Persian, tapestry and crewel yarns, canvas, belts with buckles, pillows, bag frames, and needlepoint books.

If NEPO pens are not available at your needlepoint shop, they can get them through their wholesaler or you can write to Sanford Corp., Bellwood, Ill. 60104, Att: Mary Lewis, Consumer Service Division, for information.

Hardware store

A good square and a "keyhole" saw with interchangeable blades are always useful.

Art store

ARTHUR BROWN, 2 West 46 Street, New York City 10036

A camera lucida for enlarging and reducing drawings and a light table or tracing box can be purchased here, besides other regular art supplies mentioned in this book. $10 minimum order by mail.

UTRECHT LINENS, INC., 33 35th Street, Brooklyn, New York 11232 for mail order. (New York store, 32 Third Avenue)

Excellent mail order house with savings on quantity orders of art supplies. Minimum order $15.

NOTE: Tapestry, also a good yarn, is sold in some shops rather than Persian. However, the latter is more widely distributed and has a wider color selection.

KEUFFEL & ESSER CO., Morristown, N.J. 07960

Send for graph sheet selection guide. Square grids (squares to the inch) come in 20, 16, 12, 10, 8, 6, 5, to the inch in both tracing and regular paper.

13 to the inch graph paper can be found in stationery and five and ten cent stores. It is sold as 5 squares to the centimeter.

A magnifying glass that hangs on a string around your neck can be useful for petit point or any fine canvas work. It can be purchased at any optical store.

Photostats

Fig. 17, photostat (chapter 34, Enlarging—Photostat, Lucida) by Active Photo Co., Inc.

All other photostats in this book are by F. & L. Photo Copy, 311 E. 47 St. New York City 10017

F. & L. price list (mail orders filled; large photos will be mailed in tubes)

Negatives and positives are the same price.

PHOTOSTAT PRINTS

	8½ x 11	11 x 14	14 x 18	18 x 24
Matte	$1.15	$1.40	$2.30	$2.70
Gloss	1.55	2.10	4.60	5.40

Reverse—$1.50 Additional
From Transparency—$1.50 Additional
From 35mm Transparency—$2.50 Additional
Perspective on request—Minimum $1.50

ENLARGEMENTS

Prices of materials are approximate, and subject to change.

8 x 10	$1.75	20 x 40	$ 9.00
11 x 14	2.50	30 x 40	10.50
16 x 20	4.50	30 x 50	14.00
20 x 30	6.50	40 x 50	18.00

Other sizes on request

56
Wool Chart

This wool chart shows you how much yarn it takes for a given area. It is generous in its estimate.

Canvas Area to be filled in (Squares)	Continental Stitch (Skeins)	Basket Weave Stitch (Skeins)	Half-Cross Stitch (Skeins)
4″ x 4″	1	1	1
6″ x 6″	2	2	1
8″ x 8″	3	3	2
10″ x 10″	4	4	3
12″ x 12″	5	6	4
14″ x 14″	6	8	5
18″ x 18″	10	13	8
20″ x 20″	13	15	10
22″ x 22″	16	19	12
24″ x 24″	19	22	14
27″ x 27″	24	28	18
30″ x 30″	30	34	22
32″ x 32″	34	39	25
34″ x 34″	38	44	29
(Oblongs)			
4″ x 6″	1	1	1
5″ x 7″	2	2	1
6″ x 8″	2	2	2
7″ x 66″	15	18	12
8″ x 10″	3	3	2
10″ x 12″	4	5	3
16″ x 20″	10	12	8
18″ x 24″	14	17	11
18″ x 27″	16	19	12
20″ x 27″	18	21	14
24″ x 36″	28	33	22
24″ x 42″	33	38	25

Reprinted by permission from Dorothy Sara, *Key to Needlepoint* (New York: Key Publishing House, 1967). (Basket weave estimate added.)

A 1 oz. skein is approximately 40 yards of 3-ply Persian yarn. For number of yards to 1-inch square (or 100 stitches) see chapter 15, page 55.

A 4.2 gram skein is approximately 7 yards. See chapter 44, page 177.

Convert color shapes into the number of 1-inch graph squares, half squares, and quarter squares to figure yardage needed.

For outlines count every 100 squares for each 1½ yards.

Bibliography

Hanley, Hope. *Needlepoint.* New York: Scribner's, 1964.

Gartner, Louis J., Jr. *Needlepoint Design.* New York: William Morrow & Co., Inc., 1970.

Mary Martin's Needlepoint. New York: William Morrow & Co., Inc., 1969.

Perrone, Lisbeth. *The New World of Needlepoint.* New York: Random House, 1972.

Silvia Sidney's Needlepoint Book. New York: Van Nostrand Reinhold, 1968.

Index